STEI
FIST

or

VELVET
GLOVE?

How to accelerate your career
in Management and become a
Champion for Justice

Alasdair J. Ross

Fisher King Publishing

STEEL FIST OR VELVET GLOVE?

Copyright © 2017 ALASDAIR J. ROSS

Fisher King Publishing Ltd,
The Studio,
Arthington Lane,
Pool in Wharfedale,
LS21 1JZ,
England.
www.fisherkingpublishing.co.uk

A CIP catalogue record of this book is available from the British Library
Print ISBN 978-1-910406-64-9

CONTENTS

Acknowledgements   1

How to Read This Book   5

Foreword   7

Why You Should Read This Book   13

   1.   Understanding Your Why   21

   2.   Values   42

   3.   So You Think You've Got Potential?   63

   4.   The Trouble With The System   82

   5.   Developing Your Management Tool-Kit   101

   6.   What Do You Mean, Delegate?   121

   7.   Developing Performance   143

   8.   The 3 R's   169

Conclusion   193

ACKNOWLEDGEMENTS

I wish to thank the following:

Wendy Hornack in Maui for the bi-weekly phone calls when I started this journey and her help to fine tune my ECC; Jim Jordon from Coaching Solutions for holding me accountable; Jill Bode for helping me see things in a different way; and those who contributed stories to help contextualise my thoughts: Phil Berg, Russell Sawdon, Jim Jordon, Emma Barugh, Ian Kinnery, Nigel Morgan and Julian Lewis.

In addition, my thanks to all those people with whom I have had the honour to interact and who have given me the experiences to help shape me and define my desire and purpose to 'make a difference!'

I also wish to thank my mother in particular and my siblings for helping me to become the person I am today.

And finally, to my wife, Julie, for believing in me and putting up with my need to follow the next shiny bright object.

HOW TO READ THIS BOOK?

The problem with management books are that many are bought and not read at all. Plenty are started but rarely read in their entirety for a multitude of reasons and some are read and re-read over and over again.

Physical copies are great as these are tangible, and book lovers will tell you there's just something about holding a book in their hands. That aside, downloadable kindle versions are also a great way to go, as these can be carried without the bulk of a paper version; but if the battery fails, then the book remains unread until recharge. The advantage of audio recordings of books are that they can help people get to the information contained within the book whilst on the move. The downside is that it is a linear experience, starting at the beginning and travelling through to the end. This is great for stories, but what if you want to examine a particular subject within, or jump between chapters? Then it is not quite so easy.

What type of reader are you? I personally like all of these methods, as I get a different experience from each, but I do tend to prefer a physical copy so I can highlight and underline things and make notes in the margins, which are easily returned too by a quick flick through, without the need for batteries or electricity.

Regardless of your preferred way, if you have words in front of you rather than an audio version, then I recommend you tackle the book in the following way:

- Start with looking at the front and back covers as this will give you a basic flavour of what to expect.

- Then read the abstract, in this case it's the section that is called "Why You Should Read This Book"; hopefully the reasons for this are obvious.
- The next stage should be to look at the "Contents" list. This will give you an idea of the book structure and how the chapters are laid out. Make a note of any particular chapters that pique your interest.
- Jump through each chapter to the end where there is a boxed section called "Chapter Thoughts & Actions". These give you a brief summary and some questions which may interest you to read that chapter in depth.
- Then flick through each chapter and read the various "Quotes" dotted throughout. These are relevant to the learnings contained within each of the chapters, and again will give you an insight of what is contained inside.
- If you have the time, then please read the chapters in full.
- I do suggest you make notes in the margins, turn down corners, or electronically bookmark parts you may want to review later. Highlighters are good too as they allow you to flick through the pages at a later date and pick up on key aspects without having to re-read the whole chapter.

If you are instead listening to audio, find out what button you need to bookmark sections so you can easily flick back and re-listen to them without having to fast-forward or listen to it all again from the beginning.

However you choose to read this book, I hope you get some benefit from it and that it helps you to be exceptional in your workplace. My friend Mike Macedonio recommends that you read the book from front to back, one chapter at a time. After each chapter apply the techniques from within when you get to work. Test and measure them, see what works for you, tweak and adapt them to your own style.

Most of all he says "don't tell anyone what you are doing!" just let them be surprised at how great you are as a manager of the people around you. It will get you recognised in a positive way, and who knows where the next steps on your career-path may be.

FOREWORD
By Dr. Ivan Misner

I'm often asked to do forewords for books and it was a pleasure to be able to do so for Alasdair's "Steel Fist or Velvet Glove?" especially as it tackles an interesting take on the world of management, that being that many techniques we have used in the past are still extremely relevant today. Many books have been written to try to thrust new ways to manage people upon the world, but what remains is that sometimes these new ideas are still not necessarily the best way to manage people. What we actually need to do is to reflect on what worked well in the past and adapt, innovate and update what we know to ensure the good methodologies that were effective are retained and modernised, whilst ensuring that those behaviours that are best consigned to the trash, remain there.

As we know, "Millennials", those born between the early 1980's to the late 1990's, will constitute nearly 60% of the workforce by 2030 and the view currently accepted is that the positive engagement of these people who will help shape our future is a necessary and essential goal. A truism if ever there was one, however, spending all of our efforts on teaching a 45-50-year-old to manage down will create a great manager for maybe 20 more years. Developing a 25-30-year-old to break through the traditional obstacles that are holding them back and accelerate their pathway to being a phenomenal manager and future leader, means they will give 40 years of service in that role. Perhaps the bulk of our investment is being spent in the wrong place? To make such a radical change, however, requires an insight into, and an understanding of, what the younger generations are looking for in the way they wish to conduct their service to our organisations. Their expectations and views are different to the way "work" as they seek a greater level of flexibility, responsibility, recognition and sense-of-belonging than their elders. They are often prepared to place these above monetary gain, and will move to the next job if their needs are not satisfied, which as a consequence poses a threat to staff retention, succession planning and, ultimately, business success.

This communicative and emotional disconnect of the way work is approached by the different generations still needs addressing. Even with all the technological changes that have happened in the last 40 years, and all the new ones still to come, the future workforce will still need to be managed, regardless of whether this is by a soon-to-retire Baby Boomer (born from 1946 to 1964), one of the Generation X (born between 1964 to 1979), or by an up-and-coming Millennial who is on their own journey to be one of the great managers and leaders of our future.

To help those on that journey, this book gives us a strong insight into well-founded techniques and relates them to the modern world in a way that would make either a new manager or an old-timer feel comfortable to try. Large oak trees grow from small acorns, and so the application of one small change in the way a person manages others can result in substantial changes in relatively short time-scales. This is especially important when there is a greater level of stress placed on all of us in today's fast-paced workplace; along with the continuing attitude that expects employees to adopt a long-hours work culture. This is despite the known fact that working too many hours has a negative impact on productivity and health. Many people talk about their goals to achieve a healthy work-life balance, implying equal amounts of time spent at home versus the time spent at work, but do nothing to achieve this, relying on the business itself to provide the structure for this. By achieving harmony rather than balance, it is much more likely that stress factors will be reduced and a sense of general well-being will come to the fore, creating a better work environment for the individual, but also for the company through reduced sickness absence and greater productivity.

Until the tide turns, many businesses will not take the necessary steps, continuing to adopt old-style thinking in their business model. The younger generations, however, are starting to take action to achieve a more relevant work-life harmony, where they can spend the *appropriate* amount of time at home, work or in play. In contrast to the traditional expectations of employees, Millennials are the first generation who will leave their current job for less money if they do not share in the values and work ethos of the place they are currently.

In this book, Alasdair challenges you to find your reason "why" as this will give you the belief to try some or all of the methodologies described within. So, let me ask you those questions too. Why do you want to be a manager? Do you enjoy working with people and, if so, why is that? Are you just seeking your own self-development, or do you see the role of manager as just a stepping stone to a higher pay-grade? Do you want to learn how to take control and influence others in a positive way? Is your journey about developing yourself into a great leader? It is true that all leaders have to also be great managers; and although managers can become good leaders, in many cases they are often just on the start of their journey to that end. Where are you on this journey and why? What will your story sound like when you tell it in the future?

As the founder of BNI (Business Network International) which supports over 210,000 members, in 70 countries, to generate $11.3 billion in referred closed business among themselves (May 2017), I have spent the last 3 decades telling stories to help the members understand how best to develop an effective word-of-mouth marketing programme for their own businesses. Stories are possibly the most critical means to create a construct for helping people understand more quickly. When a theory or idea is put forward and then a story created as a means to explain this, it is more quickly assimilated by the listener, or reader. This book is littered with such analogies, by those who understand how best to manage people, sharing their perspective and confirming that good techniques stand the test of time. Storytelling is so powerful because we are able to relate to the moment, and as a consequence, when faced with an employee dilemma, we will be much more likely to remember the story, the theory behind it and apply the methodology or technique effectively.

The ability to influence people to achieve positive outcomes is more essential today than ever before. This equally applies to good management, where strong people and communication skills are an essential prerequisite for developing a dynamic and cohesive team. I strongly recommend you read this book one chapter at a time. Whether you are a time-served manager or a new starter to the role of management, experiment with the techniques in this book to develop your own management tool-kit. In doing so, you will make a positive difference to those around you and become the great manager or leader you were destined to be.

Dr. Ivan Misner
Founder of BNI®

WHY YOU SHOULD READ THIS BOOK

Many people wander through their lives not really knowing their purpose, and at the end of their lives look back with the realisation they are too late to do anything about it. Mark Twain is quoted as saying *"the two most important days of your life are the day you were born, and the day you find out why"*. Yet so many of us never discover our reason "WHY".

> **"Reading a book about management isn't going to make you a good manager any more than a book about guitar will make you a good guitarist, but it can get you thinking about the most important concepts."**
> **Drew Houston**

It took me a while, but I realised that there was still an age-old issue of how to best manage the people around us. Even worse, when I spoke to my peers and those of the younger generation who are aspiring to be great, they told me they didn't actually know what was needed. They didn't have the tools and were only able to learn from their own managers, many of whom they considered poor at best. In addition, it appears that everyone wants to criticise everyone else, especially the younger generation. Bold statements like *"they have no work ethic"*, *"they are never off their damn phones"*, *"they wouldn't know a hard day's work if it slapped them in the face"* are prevalent. So if that is the so-called problem, then why are we not trying to help solve it instead of just complaining?

Personally, I detest the way many managers today deal with their people. Instead of taking a positive attitude, the pressures from the top to achieve higher performance often results in those managers reverting to type and copying the way they were managed in the past. That is not always the best way, especially if the manager of today was managed badly themselves.

What would happen then if we up-skilled the younger generation, the last of the Generation X and all of the Millennials, to be inspirational with those around them, up, down and sideways? When those people achieve a position in the company where they have the heavy responsibility of management, so long as they have been taught the right skills they will already be great managers and have the potential to inspire those around them. I firmly believe that most people would want to be seen by others as an inspirational person, someone who is revered by their peers and encouraged their boss. Is that less or more likely to result in an accelerated career path and is that person you?

Why then is it not happening now? We are meant to live in a more enlightened world where we better understand the needs of others, where we apparently know how to engage and encourage people; yet the levels of stress and depression in the workplace are increasing as each day passes. Managers are under greater pressure and demands, so it is easier to impose those pressures upon their subordinates, to bully them rather than utilising strong people skills to motivate them. It is bizarre that we do not divert our efforts to motivate and engage our employees when to do so would create a workforce that is 25% more productive and can add four times the value to an organisation. Instead, many managers try to manage by fear and control, resulting in disenfranchised staff who at best perform to half their capability.

"Treat employees like they make
a difference... and they will"
Jim Goodnight

Yet from a past perspective, such skills were less necessary when the workforce was less pressured and old-fashioned attitudes to work were more prevalent: where you didn't need to explain that starting at 9:00am meant at your desk ready to go, not arriving to hang your coat up; and where you actively took the initiative and looked for the next thing to do, not just sitting back until you were given another job. The modern employee however seeks a greater level of connection with the organisation that employs them, seeking flexibility, a sense of worth and, most critically, that their input into that organisation is listened to and valued. To do so however requires some effort as the world has moved on, changing the attitudes and expectations of everyone. To constantly hanker back to "*it wasn't like that in my day*" serves no useful purpose unless we are drawing upon experiences and past-learnings that actually add value to the situation now. We cannot change the past, nor can we live in the future; however recognising that what we do in the now and the immediate future affects where we will end up.

What will your future workplace look like, what is your vision, and what are you going to do today to affect that outcome? Managers who fail to understand this will consequently fail to engage their people, instead being left with a demotivated, stressed and disengaged workforce. Millennials, in particular, are also less willing to stay loyal to those organisations that do not value their contribution and therefore risks them leaving for pastures new. Any investment in them becomes a waste of time and money, yet putting in the effort now to make them shine will result in exceptional managers of the future who don't bully and manipulate, but do inspire. Until more recent times, becoming a manager or supervisor has been one of necessity or simply being in the right place at the right time. In many cases, the same tried and tested approach remains. However, opportunity alone does not a manager make and a common sense look at the skills needed to become an effective manager in the modern world is essential.

There is also a blasé belief and over-use of the expression "employees are your greatest asset", implying that to treat them like a piece of machinery is the only attitude required. This view is flawed, but there is no doubt that your employees are actually the most important part of your business if you wish to grow. That is not to say that being a one-man band is not rewarding, but you cannot leverage your own time without others replicating at least part of what you do. If this is true and your employees are that important, then they need to be treated as if they are valuable, notwithstanding that when things begin to go awry, peeling back the top of the glove to show a bit of steel may be necessary. It is actually just a metaphor to indicate that effective managers manage by being "firm but fair." By doing so and acknowledging the needs and expectations of the individual will ensure the psychological contract between employer and employee is strong, resulting in far more motivated, respectful and productive employees. An essential part of this is the modern manager's ability to relate to their employees, face to face, even in a world beset by instant communication, online learning and social media.

To be honest, it's important that I also explain that this book contains no extensive quantitative surveys of multiple blue-chip organisations, or even clever theories and systems that can be replicated, franchised or sold. However, this book and what I feel I must share with you, has been based on a personal journey, testing and measuring what does and does not work when managing the people you may be responsible for. It works for me and I hope that you consider what I have written as valuable, and tackle the chapters one at a time.

What I mean by that is, please read each chapter, one at a time, and try out the techniques therein. Once you have done so read the next chapter and apply something you have learned. Test and measure it, or adapt it to fit your own management style if that's what it takes to make it work. Now, some of you will and some of you won't, but I hope you learn to apply even just one small thing to improve the way you deal with your employees and, as a result, create a better workplace. One other thing, don't tell your boss that you are trying these things out. Seriously, don't. Be focussed, determined and watch the results.

I am confident that by holding your own counsel, your skills as a great manager will improve and consequently be noticed. Those who hold a position in your organisation that you aspire to are constantly looking for the talent that will replace them when they move on or retire. If you are the person that shows willing, are the one who pushes creative ideas forward without appearing disappointed when they are not utilised, gets the most out of your team and your own manager, who shows a desire to learn and grow to be the best you can be; then you will be noticed. People will then also want to be around you, to learn from you, to emulate you; and your career path into management or to the next level will be assured. Remember that you are always on a journey of improvement as it is the journey, not the destination, which is so much more important.

"Anyone who has never made a mistake has never tried anything new."
Albert Einstein

Incidentally, it's not easy to manage people – so let's get that myth out in the open for a start because, quite simply, everyone is different and each has arrived at this point in time from a different perspective, context and experience. Being a skilled manager can however become a learned skill if you are willing to embrace a different way to do things and see what works for you. What I have tried to do with this book is to share my "tool-kit" of stuff I have found to work for me with the people I have come into contact with. So if you take just one thing from this book and it helps you to better manage or motivate a person you are responsible for, then I have achieved one of my life goals; and you have just increased the tools you have in your own tool box.

Now, we all learn in different ways. Some people need to write stuff down, whilst others just read it and remember. There are those that learn from listening, and those from doing it in a practical way. Do what works for you, but please do something. Every journey of a thousand miles begins with a single step and sometimes we head in the wrong direction, but at least we're moving. On the journey, we meet people who give us new directions, we overcome obstacles, and grow with that knowledge and experience. Making mistakes is okay, just let's ensure we don't make the same mistake over and over again. The alternative is to sit on our backsides and expect the world to revolve around us; in the scheme of things and our limited time on this planet, do we really have the right to be that presumptuous?

So, about using this book to help grow your knowledge and experience. Well I've read and listened to many management books, articles and journals, attended seminars and webinars, and spent many a long hour deliberating and discussing with my peers what works and what doesn't. The only thing I do know for certain is that what works for one person won't necessarily work for another, and that you glean less than 10% of usable information from most management books the first time you read them. This is because we can't take in too much information at any one time, we rarely take action with the information we have assimilated, and some of the information is just not relevant to us at this moment in time.

However you want this book to work for you, go for it. Read it all in one go, in chapters bit by bit, or dip in and out of sections you've noted in the index. What I would ask is that if you find something that works for you, please share it. The more people that adopt good practice, the more likely we are collectively to develop happy workplaces. To paraphrase Steven R. Covey, who wrote *Seven Habits of Highly Effective People*, "if you learn something, teach it to someone else within forty-eight hours and you will gain a deeper understanding of that thing and also enrich the life of the other person". Sound advice, and so I implore you to share what you may learn in this book, whether it be a single technique, a phrase, or you allow it to totally transform your management style.

That is why you should read this book. It is full of ways to build your own tool-kit, to develop your own brilliant style of inspiring people who want to give more of themselves. It offers you an insight as well as techniques for managing both those you are in charge of and those who manage you. Being a great communicator will give you the edge over others. Learning how to best support and motivate another to excel will get you noticed in the right way. Developing your people by being an exceptional manager yourself will influence future generations because they will copy you, and if you are the best, then they too will be great. This is what I passionately believe is the role of the manager; not just to get the tasks done, but to also operate at the coal-face to build effective teams of highly motivated people who enjoy the work they do. What do you want to be remembered for?

Chapter 1
UNDERSTANDING YOUR WHY

Perhaps you have picked up this book because you like the cover, or maybe it was recommended to you by your mentor, or just maybe you want to understand how to become a great manager. If it is the latter, and I sincerely hope this is the case, then you need to discover your Emotionally Charged Connection (E.C.C.), in effect to understand your "WHY".

Explore why you do what you do, why you are who you are in your personal and business life; why being a manager is so important to you, why you actually bother to have a business; and if you have one, then why that matters to you and those you service or build products for. To help you further understand your own reasons, I'd highly recommend a book by Simon Sinek called, "*Start With Why*". His "Golden Circle" may help you to focus on helping your own business or organisation in which you work to understand the WHY, but the message is just as relevant and powerful on a personal level too.

It took me many years before I understood this and found my own why. That didn't mean I wasn't subconsciously looking for it for many years. However, it wasn't until a moment in time in November 2014 in Los Angeles when I discovered my own why and all became so much clearer. That was when I attended a three-day training programme expecting to learn lots of processes, with tips and tricks on how to build a more powerful referral word-of-mouth marketing system for my business, but it turned out to be so much more.

The Golden Circle

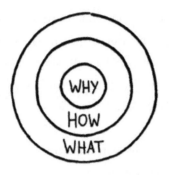

What

Every organization on the planet knows WHAT they do. These are products they sell or the services they offer.

How

Some organizations know HOW they do it. These are the things that make them special or set them apart from their competition.

Why

Very few organizations know WHY They do what they do. WHY is not about making money. That's a result. It's a purpose, cause or belief. It's the very reason your organization exists.'

Until that moment, I had been running my human resource consultancy, We do HR Limited, which I had established in March 2003 as a one-man-band and was doing okay, or so I thought. Lots of failures and mistakes on the journey – and taking the odd risk – had my business growing to the point where I employed three full-time staff, servicing around a hundred clients of all sizes across the UK. So, the value of expanding my years of referral marketing knowledge (through being a member of BNI®) to the next level, and tagging on some development and training seemed a great idea. Better still, this might seriously help me to grow my business to the next level. I wanted more, but didn't know how to get there. The reality of that week was very different and changed my life, and my business, forever.

I discovered that I had spent most of my working life pushing on doors to find the way forward, always looking for the next best thing to help make the leap to the next level. My wife, Julie, describes this as me: "looking for the next bright shiny thing that will make us millionaires, but in reality is just another distraction". Needless to say, when I said I was attending the *Asentiv®* (formerly *Referral Institute®*) programme, she considered this to be just another one of those distractions.

I am glad to say that she was on this occasion totally wrong as I went through what felt like "three days of open-heart surgery to have my eyes opened." I discovered that my mind was cleared of white-noise and that I knew exactly what I was here to do. As an aside, I hadn't realised I had a head full of white-noise or static until it was gone, but as a consequence, I found myself mentally and spiritually grounded with a certainty of what my purpose on this little planet was all about. I cannot express how grateful I am to Eddie Esposito, Dawn Lyons and Mike Macedonio of *Asentiv®* for helping me open the right door at the right time to a whole world of possibilities by helping me find my E.C.C.

I have always believed that the journey of our lives, the interactions, events and drama that we experience, shapes who we are. I also believed that the person I was before November 2014, had been shaped more by recent business knowledge rather than things that had happened earlier in my life. I'm not a great one for living in history as it isn't somewhere I can affect. The discovery that my parents from an early age had been hugely influential in setting my beliefs, morals and standards, and setting me on my path, had been forgotten. For now, with that in mind, I realised I needed to go much further back than I felt comfortable with.

I was born in 1962 in the Salvation Army Nursing Home in Partick, Glasgow. I was the third child of what would be four siblings; yet I often wonder if my parents brought the wrong baby home as I am of a totally different character to the others, being extremely extrovert, always positive and I never stop talking.

Times in Glasgow were tough; despite having a very young family to support, Mum and Dad were also obligated to look after an elderly aunt who lived with us. On top of that, as a proud Scottish family, we were expected to do as we were told by Grandma Ross – a real Matriarch – which meant that when she said jump, we all asked "how high". Regardless, my parents held true to their beliefs and high moral standards. We were taught respect, the meaning of hard work, and that to do well required dedication. These traits were to stand me in good stead across the future and there have been many occasions where I have drawn upon our Clan Motto to spit in the eye of adversity, "Spem Successus Alit" which means "Success Nourishes Hope".

My father was a Chartered Mechanical and Electrical Engineer, and left Glasgow to become the General Manager at Dunlop in Speke, Liverpool. From then I grew up in an old, large house with draughty windows, no central heating and an outside toilet. This improved over time as my father

renovated the house bit-by-bit, and as kids we were fortunate to be able to run wild in a large garden without fear of being run over on the road. We did not have much spare money and personal technology was non-existent, so instead we learnt to explore our imagination to occupy ourselves. My mother, although a qualified Teacher, was a stay-at-home mum as my father did not believe the mother should work except to raise the kids, and he provided her with a house-keeping allowance to do this. The world was a different place in those days, but it didn't mean those things were bad or wrong, they were just not the same as today.

I have no doubt that my father would have embraced the developments in people management, as in the early 70's he brought home tape-programmes around motivation, brain-storming and communication skills. I was very interested in these and would listen to them too, so maybe even then my path was being established. I was close to my father and he taught me how to play golf, to have a sense of humour and he also shared his thoughts on management. As was the trend in the 1970's, there seemed to always be a dinner party going on in the house and I was inspired by Dad to network and communicate with people even then. It was where I learnt all about social networking — and no, I don't mean Facebook, Twitter or LinkedIn! Sadly, such positive influences were to come to an abrupt halt as pancreatic cancer took him away in June 1975. I was 12 years old.

I feel it important to clarify that I had a great childhood and my mother has done a fabulous job, bringing up four young children by herself. However, the parental influences on my mother's childhood pre-World War II can have a lasting impact upon the behavioural traits of the Silent Generation, which is then transposed upon later generations. I have no doubt my mother believed she was acting in my best interests, but she defaulted to an extremely strong matriarch who exercised great control over every aspect of my life, as her mother had done before. The start of this was in the spring of 1975 when I said goodbye to my father in an ambulance before he was rushed to hospital. Despite my pleading, my mother would not let me see my father again even though it was three months before he died. After all, I was "just a little boy", "wouldn't understand" and it was "for my own good". My little sister and I were also not allowed to go to my father's funeral for much the same reason. As I grew up through my teenage years, there would be many occasions where my mother would exert her control over my actions, holding me back and embarrassing me in front of others. Control, dominance and threats of "if you don't do as I tell you … (insert relevant consequence)" were frequent. This set the tone for a trend that would continue for many years of "do as you are told, I know best!"

Now we all deal with things in a different way. My youngest sister Katie, was only 10 when dad died, and being the baby of the family, did everything she was told, as at that time she was unable to rationalise what had happened in any other way. It is only now that the impact of my mothers' "best-intentioned" parenting has been realised by her; but that is another story. My eldest sister Alison escaped the controlling influences and left for Oxford University. My older brother David, a troubled 15-year-old introvert, sought solace in alcohol. This latter factor created many issues as my mother would frequently threaten to throw him out of the house, which was not something I could cope with having lost my dad. There were many occasions on a Friday evening when I would come home from Scouts to find my mother out at a dinner party, my sister Katie at friends overnight and the house locked up in darkness. Climbing the drainpipe at the rear and breaking into my bedroom was the only solution to again find my brother slumped in his bed covered in vomit. Fearful of the repercussions, I would sort that mess out, such that when my mother came home in the early hours and went to bed, she would wake the next morning blissfully unaware there had been a problem. I could not allow any further break-up of the family, so even then it appears that I was fighting for the underdog.

As a teenager growing up in the 1970's in Britain, I was subjected to many differing attitudes from those around me towards other people from different races, creeds and cultures, especially homosexuals and ethnic minorities. Even though these attitudes were normal at the time, I was incongruent with these views and so challenged those that made derogatory comments. My protests fell on deaf ears, yet I am thankful that globally we have now evolved some way to enlightenment; but I'm still convinced that many people have just suppressed their views rather than having changed them, as recent events have shown racism, sexism – and generally being bigoted – to still be prevalent among some people. Back in the 1970's, I was conflicted with those influences that tried to mould me to be the same as everyone else. It would have been easy to keep my head down and say nothing, but that was and still is not who I am. Unfortunately, the consequences of openly sharing your opinion is that you stand out and therefore become a target. "What doesn't kill you makes you stronger" became my unspoken mantra, and it was to be many years later before I realised that standing up for others was my reason for being here.

Now, before you think this is a sob story, it's not. As a youngster, I didn't know that the way I was being treated was wrong, nor am I looking to blame anyone, it was just the way it was. My recollections were of a good and happy childhood, but there is no doubt in my mind now, that being belittled and bullied, deliberately or sub-consciously, regardless of how subtly it was carried out, has a lasting impact upon the psyche. What actually matters is how you deal with the cards you are dealt. Some of you may remember a Fisher Price toy called a "Weeble", with a weighted and rounded bottom so that when you pushed it over, it just rolled back upright again. The marketing phrase was simple – "Weebles Wobble But They Don't Fall Down" and was one of those sayings that sticks. So I made a decision early on to be a Weeble and get back up again, and again, and again. There are many sayings about being resilient and bouncing back; like General George A. Custer's saying "It matters not how many times you are pushed down, but how many times you get back up again." Over the years to follow, I was to find that bouncing back from the put-downs was to stand me in good stead.

Despite going to a private grammar school, without a father figure to aspire to, my studies suffered. Fortunately, I hold a strong belief that it is not necessarily about the education itself but the people you associate with that matters in preparing you for the future. I like to think my parents believed that too and sent me there for that reason.

"The person you will be five years from now is totally dependent on the books you read and the people you associate with"

Bill O'Brien

In the summer of 1979 I reached another major crossroads in my life when a brown envelope with my 'O' Level results arrived in the post. My mother stayed in bed reading the newspaper as she told me later she knew my results were going to be bad. I suppose it hadn't occurred to her that she should have thought about that while I was going through my schooling, but then again, she had her own demons to deal with.

The way I wanted to deal with my issues was to get out of education and take a different path. Mum said I couldn't wait to run away, which looking back now I suppose I did. However, Physics is essential if you want to be a Marine Navigator as its application is critical for ship stability and operations. I had just scraped an 'E' grade, avoiding an 'F' for FAIL by only a few percentage points. I was distraught. This was my dream and it was my fault, if only I had realised then that you have to work at the things that matter if you want to succeed. Thank goodness I was an indestructible Weeble, and so for the first time of many occasions, I took control of my own destiny.

Phoning the shipping companies to tell them my grades was the first difficult step in taking responsibility for my actions. One by one, Cunard, BP and Shell gave a very abrupt "sorry we cannot take you with a fail at Physics, goodbye". The fourth and last call I made was to Charlie Turner, the Personnel Officer at P&O. I fully expected the same response, but dialled the number with a grim determination that at least I would sound confident regardless of the outcome. There I was again standing at the crossroads of the journey of life and all I now needed was the signpost to show me the way. With fingers crossed and bated breath I listened to him ask, "That's very interesting Mr. Ross, what do you intend to do about it?" Maybe I recognised that this was another early management influence, as he gave me options and an opportunity to voice my opinions instead of being dismissive.

How easy it would have been to just roll over and give up; but I replied with a steady voice, "I'm re-sitting my Physics exam in November, if I pass do I still have a chance?" Reassured by an affirmative response, I realised in that very moment that each and every one of us holds the key to our own destiny and in my case, it was down to me and me alone. If I wanted this, I'd better do something about it. I took over the dining room table and got studying. Less than 3-months later, I re-sat my exam and increased my grade from an 'E' to a 'B'. Looking back, I enjoyed school but I didn't apply myself and it nearly cost me dearly. Since that phone call and the realisation of the potential lost opportunity, I've never devalued the power of education in any form and I've never stopped learning since.

In January 1980, I left home to sail the world for four-and-a-half years with the British Merchant Fleet. At the time, I found it remarkable that from five thousand miles away my mother's influences were significantly less. I was finally able to be my own person. Life was great, I had my own money, I three-times circumnavigated the globe visiting most of the sub-continents, and met some wonderful people from many different cultures, and I expanded my belief that I was a "global human being" sharing a commonality with all mankind, not just those from Scotland.

Such views were not prevalent in the early 1980's and I found in general there was an undercurrent of disrespect from my fellow officers towards the crew and others from a different race, creed or sexual orientation. I don't mean the issuing of orders; the hierarchical structure was necessary for the safety of the ship and its occupants. I'm referring to a small number of my colleagues who considered that excessive control, belittlement and coercion were the effective tools of good people management. Putting another person down just to make themselves look more important seemed the order of the day and I was expected to follow suit, but I was again in conflict with this attitude.

As a Deck Officer on Watch, I was in charge of the crew. Based on orders from the Chief Officer, my manager, I had to task them with their work and supervise its effective conclusion. I always showed a genuine interest in the crew, to hear about their culture and their families, and felt my relationship with them was good. Some of my colleagues however did not and treated them with disdain, putting them down in front their friends and work-mates. I challenged this behaviour but to no avail, as their vitriol was then turned on me. What I really could not understand was that we were on a tin box with 35-40 people on it, hundreds of miles away from land or help. If you bully someone and make them feel worthless, would they be less or more likely to come to your assistance if a genuine emergency occurred? This applied just as much then as it does today; if you treat people badly, they don't work as effectively.

I'm sure that my stance to fight for the underdog, rather than condone the actions of bullies, was not a factor in the decision to make me redundant – but looking back, perhaps my forthright attitude did result in the loss of my first vocational career and leave me seeking a new challenge.

My brother David had been in the Northumbria Police for a while and encouraged me to join up. A strong, self-disciplined organisation that saw service to the public as vital was an appealing prospect and I thought this was somewhere I could make a difference. Three months later, I was a fresh-faced Constable in Durham, 200 miles away from my mother's influence, much to her annoyance. I believed I was taking a role in society which would serve the public and make a difference, however, three years later I began to wonder why I was there. To a certain extent, I did change people's lives and helped the communities I was involved in, and as a bonus I developed my skills as an effective communicator through dealing with many different situations from empathy to hostility. Deep down, I knew I felt myself at odds with many of my colleagues once again.

It began within a few months of joining and the Miner's Strike was in full swing. The mining communities were full of proud people, with generations of them working in the pits and now standing for what they believed in. Laudable, except for the fact they were not being paid and emotions were running high. To control the violence, hundreds of Police Officers in full riot gear were brought in from all over the country. From the cordon-line, the officers would hold up a pay slip and taunt the mob of miners with the hefty overtime they were earning. Pumped up and full of bravado, those officers in heavy protection were eager to use their batons and shields to "control this menace" through a heavy-handed approach. Even then, this form of management could not get the best from people. Now it would be unfair to say everyone behaved that way, but there were enough who held a bad attitude and caused more issues than the reason for the strike. "Behaviour begets behaviour" and as local law enforcement, I was one of those left to deal with the aftermath of domestic violence that ensued. The positive takeaway from those early years, was that I developed the ability to handle all manner of conflict even when it was up close and personal.

It was not all about the violence but more about control; the saying goes "in order to be to be a good copper you need to act like a good villain". This attitude is not always correct and despite being a "family", many would close ranks on other officers, often seeking opportunities to gain the upper hand. There are too many occasions to tell, but suffice to say that instead of entering a profession where I expected exemplary conduct towards colleagues, I found an undertone of bullying and coercion to be rife from all levels, and I was often on the receiving end. Being vocal, I had my say, which did not go down well and resulted in some difficult conversations with my superiors, but fundamentally nothing changed. Now it could be argued that high spirits were necessary to counter the stresses we faced on the streets, but I have always believed that you have the ability to control your attitude – and therefore your behaviour – from the moment you get up each day. I still believe this to be true, so who you are going to be today is about a decision that you make when you look in the mirror. I made the decision that I would not become a clone but would exert whatever influence I could to change attitudes. As part of this I became a Tutor Constable and trained new recruits, setting the standards for excellence and teaching them that getting positive results was easily achievable if you learnt to treat people in the right way.

"There are only two ways to influence human behaviour, you can manipulate it or inspire it"
Simon Sinek

Little did I know the challenges I faced during a decade of loyal service, was just part of a journey, the next phase of which was about to manifest itself. In August 1994, I was faced with six drunk and drugged-up young men who had made their decision to "have a copper" that evening. I was the target and suffered with a back-injury that would leave me with everyday pain, restricted movement and finally medical retirement 18 months later. I made a decision that I would never allow this injury to stop me from living life to the fullest and achieving what I needed to.

Two vocational careers down and wondering where my life was going to, I met Norma Taylor who organised the Executive Job Club and began to search for my next opportunity. She gave me hope that despite missing out on University I could compete against my peers who had degrees and showed me my real worth. Soon afterwards, I was employed at a media company that specialised in news, weather, traffic and travel supplies to the radio and television industry.

This was a fast-paced, reactive industry, punching out 30-second traffic bulletins live on air from ground and Cessna aircraft above the roads. Mistakes were easy to make and resulted in the six Area Managers having to handle irate clients who reiterated that "no matter how good you are as a broadcaster, you are only as good as your last bulletin"! With many staff being creative types with large egos, telling them they were not good enough generated a huge level of conflict and emotional tantrums. Poor managers all too often revert to type and use coercive bullying tactics to try to justify their roles, something I would take responsibility for dealing with over the next fourteen months.

In my region, I established a centre for excellence, in profit and with staff that wanted to work and play hard. It was fun and we shared a common goal to be the best in the UK, which we were. This was recognised by Head Office and I was asked to help shape the remaining regions in a similar vein. One by one, the Area Managers were moved on because they were not fit for purpose and I stepped up to UK Operations Manager. I was now working closely with the Board to grow the company to over 250 employees and started my Master's Degree in Strategic Human Resource Management to support my operational skill set. Aged thirty-eight, I was at University, albeit part-time, whilst juggling a 60-hours-per-week job.

The company was growing rapidly and having gained a large capital injection to help take us to the next level, I was then part of the Operating Board. Shortly afterwards we had a new CEO thrust upon us who applied his own style of management and leadership. I was in an industry I loved and was good at, but again was faced with institutionalised bullying as the CEO started to strip out the number of employees around the six regional offices. Halving the number of employees was the objective and he didn't care how it was achieved, so I did what I do best to help those who left. My goal was to do this in a way that didn't demean them.

I was also starting to realise that in every job I had been in, as well as in all the businesses that were peripheral to those, as clients or suppliers, there was an undercurrent of bad management which left employees feeling less worthy. It was time to make a difference, so I seized the chance and left corporate London to start my own human resource consultancy in the North East.

The biggest downside of starting your own business is that it helps a lot if you have business contacts in the area you set up. I didn't! I also didn't have the same level of support that is available today for new start-ups and I mentioned earlier that Facebook and Twitter didn't even exist. That aside, I learnt how to network, build my contacts and reputation, steadily growing my revenue streams. It was satisfying and I was enjoying myself with the freedom that comes from being your own boss. I was still working as many hours for less money initially but spent quality time seeing my kids grow up and, in the businesses I was working with, I felt I was making a real difference. I found that I was dealing with an increasing number of issues relating to poor communication and over-bearing conduct towards others in those companies; interestingly, it was not always the managers who were at fault. The next 11 years were focused on increasing the number of clients who I could support more effectively and change their culture, such that they themselves would grow more successful.

That brings me back to my trip to Los Angeles where I discovered my "WHY" and everything became so much clearer.

The final piece of the jigsaw, was that the keynote speaker at the BNI®

Global Convention that year was Jack Canfield and he helped me focus on what to do with my purpose, my reason why.

I have already mentioned the time I have devoted to growing my own personal knowledge through books, audio and seminars (to name a few resources), and I am sure many of you have too. It is not about what we hear or say that matters, but what we do; we are all faced with a choice to act or not. That experience in November 2014 was simply a case of me being in the right place at the right time and where I first made a decision and that I would then take action to implement it. I am grateful that I was able to discover my purpose, and in that respect I realised that I am a *"Champion for Justice"* and all of the jobs and experiences throughout my life were training me for my mission to fight <u>for</u> the underdog. That helped me make the decision, and then all I needed to do was to follow through, which I did with total conviction. That came from the realisation that all throughout my life I have challenged authority for the greater good. I detest bad employers and bad employees with equal vehemence and my purpose, in however many years I have left, is to make a real and tangible difference in that arena.

> **"If you can tune into your purpose and really align with it, setting goals so that your vision is an expression of that purpose, then life flows much more easily."**
> **Jack Canfield**

As aforementioned, what particularly concerns me is that in our so called enlightened world, there is more bullying of people taking place with resultant work-related stress, costing the economy millions, than ever before. How can that be? The answer is in how we manage the people we have a responsibility for.

It is well-documented that employees who are engaged in the workplace will give 25% more of themselves. That means 25% more effort, productivity, and commitment, which in turn by default means greater profitability; yet an employee who is disengaged and dis-incentivised will work at around half their capability. I am constantly amazed that employers will not spend time trying to engage their staff but would rather create a workplace that is mediocre at best and toxic at worst. On a basic Cost Benefit Analysis, not engaging your people is like setting fire to a bag full of £20 notes, which doesn't make any sense at any level.

Discovering my purpose now meant I could accelerate the ability to affect more people in a positive way, and know why I was doing it. If you are to take the most from this book to gain the understanding of how to be a better manager of people, then perhaps a good place to start is with finding your own reason why. However you find it, I guarantee that discovering your own personal why will forever shape and enrich your life going forward.

I implore you to take at least one thing from this book, one technique, one way to speak to people in a more positive way, or just a sense that you can manage an employee or colleague better and get stronger results. Perhaps you could make significant or minor changes to the way your business works so that everyone benefits; but most of all, my desire is that we stamp out workplace bullying once and for all. Whether you are hugely experienced or just starting along your career path, becoming a great manager will not only influence and inspire those around you, but will give you a sense of reward and eliminate bullying as a consequence – because exceptional managers don't need to coerce or intimidate others to get great results from them. I hope that this book inspires you take the steps on that journey with me and help to make that difference.

Chapter Thoughts and Actions:

• What are the things that matter to you the most?

• Reflect on "who" you are in order to discover your "why".

• Ask yourself; "what is my passion?"

• Review the story of your own life so far and consider how powerful those experiences could be if shared with others.

Chapter 2
VALUES

Definition:

Important and lasting beliefs or ideals, shared collectively by members of a culture or organisation, about what they consider to be good or bad, desirable or otherwise that influence their behaviour and attitude.

Before we start telling others how to be better, it is probably important that we understand ourselves to a greater depth. In doing so we will be able to communicate much more effectively because we will understand others with clarity and certainty. If we know how another person feels, what they believe in, how they like to be spoken to, or how they may react in certain situations, it is reasonable that they would be more responsive to what we ask them to do.

This is even more important when we look at the issues between Generation X and Generation Y, or as they are more commonly called, Millennials. Which of these are you? The more experienced older person managing the younger, dynamic, hungry individual; or the person on the receiving end? A failure by either person to grasp the core values of the other, creates a communicative and emotional disconnect, which at best results in a failure to achieve objectives and at worst creates direct conflict.

To start with: if we are privileged enough to understand a person's core values, do we know our own? If not, then what matters to us may be in direct conflict with the other person, and asking someone to carry out a task that is in contravention of their beliefs or values, will probably result in them refusing to do the task, or making a half-hearted attempt at doing it. A conflict with your values will usually create an internal, and sometimes external, emotional response. Think about it, if you are the person being told to do something, how does that make you feel? How do you react? Both you and your manager, who after all is just trying to just get the job done, have an opportunity to decide how the situation will work out. How then will you communicate with your manager and how will they speak to you? Unfortunately, we don't walk around with a tattoo on our forehead telling others what our values are, so we need to understand how to recognise these in others. What therefore is a core value?

To start with, everyone has a value-system, even if they don't realise it or know what their values are part of it. Core values are the key drivers that determine how an individual perceives the world around them and they affect that person's behaviour and conduct. They are of great importance to the individual determining their principles, morals and/or standards of what is considered appropriate to them, further influencing their judgement on what is and what isn't important. Values are developed over time as a person grows, based on the rules and moral compass established by their parents. This often includes projected prejudices (which can be aligned or contrary to how the individual is now) and from the actual experiences the individual has undergone as they grow up. In reality, understanding your main five core values would be sufficient as it would not be sensible to try to juggle too many at the same time – these could create internal conflict when faced with a decision or dilemma.

Values are usually deep-seated, emotionally anchored and hard to change. They can however alter where there has been a "life-event", usually one with an emotional impact that makes someone re-evaluate themselves. For example, where a younger person places exhilarating risk-taking, such as high-altitude extreme skiing, as something they value most because of the fun they have and the adrenaline bursts they get from it; then everything else they do in life would be focussed on earning the money to be able to do this. If this was the case, then this activity would form the basis for their key core values, i.e. fun and risk-taking. They will place this activity above everything else and to suddenly stop doing it would not necessarily be easy. However, getting married or having a child may be the emotional event which replaces this core value with one now based around family – but not always. It may take a serious accident, a life-event, to generate the necessary emotional impact on that individual to make the shift in the core value, so that when given a choice the individual would not go skiing but would rather spend time with his family, because of the risks to their health. Now, the person may still place the fun of skiing as important to them, but less so resulting in them choosing the lower level less-dangerous runs instead.

> **"Values aren't buses...**
> **They're not supposed to get you anywhere.**
> **They're supposed to define who you are."**
> **Jennifer Crusie**

Let's think about this a little more, as understanding values is critical to understanding strong positive communication, which you need if you are to be an effective manager. On a personal level, it could be the driver that makes you run the London Marathon every year to raise money for that local charity that is so important to you; or why you help out each year at a homeless shelter on Christmas Day; or perhaps why you became a counsellor to help others suffering from some level of abuse. Maybe you devote a lot of your time to be a School Governor or Chair of the local PTA to give back because you want the children following in your footsteps to be given the best chance at education. You may be a volunteer at a local youth group, Scouts or Girl Guides, because those experiences that developed your own team spirit and self-worth deserve to be shared among our future generations. What makes you "give" selflessly of yourself rather than spend your time taking from society, allowing others to do it for you, or worse still spending most of your non-working life watching the dirge of television programmes that add little or no value to anyone or anything?

On a business level, most business owners (note I didn't say employees) don't really know why they do what they do. They think it's about making money, but often that is a by-product and we are actually driven by other reasons. If you are such a business owner, ask yourself why you started this particular business? Was it a hobby that became bigger than intended taking on its own self-fulfilling prophesy such that you just had to do it? Or was it a fantastic idea stumbled upon by accident, and through support and encouragement from your family you decided to give it a go? Perhaps you took over the "family business" by default but are not really passionate about it because the reasons you are doing it are not the reasons the business was started by your parents and you don't share their passion for it.

Your ECC however is deeply rooted to your core values: the very fibre of

45

your being that makes you do those extra things that others don't seem to want to do. Values are not easy to define and if you ask most people they will struggle to tell you what theirs are. Once you understand them however, you will see how they shape you as a person, in the decisions that you make, the stances that you take and how you live your life. Brian Tracey in his book "*Time Power*" explains how we can determine our values through our decisions about how we live our life. Let me paraphrase him in explanation.

Take three core values that may be important to you, for now let's say – **Health – Family – Career** – and if you had to choose, which of these three is the MOST important to you? I accept all may be important, but which one would you pick over the others?

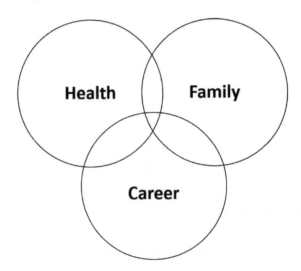

Let's say your health is the most important thing to you. You eat well and sensibly, you exercise regularly, have all the nice but not-so-good stuff in moderation. You look after yourself. The problem is that the exercise routine means you are training on the evening when your daughter is at her first school play and wants you there, but you have to train, it's important to you. You've made a commitment to yourself and you need to stay disciplined. If you don't, perhaps you won't be fit enough to run the marathon you've set your heart on, so you don't go to the play, you place your fitness before your family! How did that go down then?

Worse still it may be the other way around and you work long hours to pay the bills, eating poorly at the wrong times, you drink too much and are overweight. After all, you are the bread-winner in the house and have to work this hard or you will not be able to provide the life-style your family crave. You see it as important, yet you are exhausted and it is only a matter of time before you have a heart-attack. By not placing health high enough on your list, you may end up debilitated or dead – how will that help your family as you may now not be able to earn any money?

If it's family that is the most important thing to you, what happens when your boss offers you that once in a life-time career opportunity, but taking it will mean you have to spend every Monday to Friday away from home? Do you choose the career move for the money, the opportunity, the power and status that it will give you? Do you tell yourself that you worked hard to get those qualifications doing all the rotten jobs to gain the experience, that you deserve this break and just how much that £65,000 raise will help you and your family to have the life you dreamed of? After all, with that sort of money, you can hire a nanny to look after the kids! Accepting the job, however, means precious time away from your loved ones.

Is this a dilemma or not? If your number one core value is "Family" then you will put them above everything else, including your job. For example, what happens when you are working late (as is often the case) and one of your children has an accident and you need to leave work? You ask your boss for the time off and he says "no, the project you are working on is too important and needs finishing tonight, if you leave, then you are fired!" What are you going to do? If work is more important you will stay, if your family is more important you will go and trust that you will find another job. Tough call? Absolutely. But what if your boss understood what mattered to you – would they treat you differently on that occasion and allow you to go? Have you taken the time to share with your boss the reasons why family is so important to you? Has your boss or manager taken the time to get to know you and have you been open enough to tell them. I'm not saying you have to be best buddies but they aren't mind-readers either.

I was faced with a difficult dilemma, of a similar nature, many years ago when working in London. As Operations Manager, I absolutely needed to be at an extremely important meeting at the BBC in Pebble Mill, Birmingham. It was the sort of meeting that would double the company turnover, employ another 75 people and secure the company's future for many years. I was a pivotal part of the negotiations. To make things easier, I was staying with my wife at my mother's house in Cheshire so I only had an hour to drive to the meeting on the Monday morning. My father-in-law was in a care home at that time and was generally unwell. We knew it was only a matter of time and had prepared ourselves for the worst. At 4:30a.m., we got the call … "you need to come now, his condition has deteriorated". I was now conflicted! Do I drive my wife the 250-mile journey back north again to Darlington, or go to the meeting and hope to make it back before he died? Work was important, but so was family. Just so you know I made the wrong call and went to the meeting. My mother drove Julie home and she made it with about 2 hours to spare; I didn't and have regretted that decision ever since. I don't mean that my wife didn't forgive me, she did eventually, even though I chose work over supporting her at a time when she needed me. What I do regret is not saying my last goodbyes to someone who was one of my best friends (even though he was my father-in-law) while he was still alive. Looking back, do I think the meeting could have gone ahead without me or even been rescheduled? Probably, but I made a decision based on what I thought was more important at that time. Given that time over again, I would have taken a different decision.

What then are the values that matter to you? All of the above three are relevant and sensible core values to have, but which one will you place above all others? They are not the only three values you should consider, but I urge you to take the time to question who you are and why you do what you do. Find your values and stick with them; trust them to guide you to make the right choices at the right time.

I discovered what values are all about and what mine were about ten years ago. "Honesty" and "Integrity", although not the only ones, are the two most important to me. People who conflict with these values create an emotional response in me and I have to challenge this. For example, when I carry out an investigation in the workplace, I am driven to uncover the truth and instinctively know when someone is lying and covering up. I am <u>driven</u> to discover the truth. When someone such as a client does something that is morally incomprehensible, I get mad and have to do something about it. Maybe it is helping and supporting then to see the correct way, or maybe it is cutting them loose and no longer servicing that client. I have to do what is right for me, or agonise and face internal conflict. In my own business, it is critical that I have employees who share my values, as in my opinion, it's the only way that works.

"Find people who share your values, and you'll conquer the world together."
John Ratzenberger

So, if we accept that values are important to us individually, then it should be easy to recognise that we need to be able to understand someone else's values or risk conflicting with them. If we get it right, it can be a powerful way to motivate people. Let me give you some examples.

You know that Peter loves the football and supporting his team; in fact, he has never missed a match in twelve years. An important match is on next Wednesday evening, but it is miles away and in order to leave work and get there on time, he would need to finish at 1p.m. or take holiday (of which he has none left). This is his passion, all he ever does is talk about supporting his team. You recognise one of his core values to be the enjoyment he gets from going to the home and away matches. You also know that there is a deadline for delivery on a project that Peter is managing and there is insufficient time for Peter to complete this and get away early. In managing this situation effectively and playing to Peter's values, you pull in extra resource and suggest the team stays back on Monday and Tuesday evenings to get the project completed. You tell Peter that if they get finished by lunchtime Wednesday, he can leave early and get to the match. Given that situation, is Peter less or more likely to put in the extra effort to manage his team to achieve the results needed?

Abigail is a great sales person, but she is struggling to close the sale and seems to have lost her mojo. She has a passion for driving fast sports cars and has set her heart on buying a Jaguar F-Type. She has been on a few test drives and talked to you about the feeling she has when people stare at her driving past with the roof down. You know she has a long way to go to raise enough bonus to buy the car of her dreams, but she has an emotional attachment (a core value) based on driving fast and the exhilaration she feels when others look at her driving. You need more sales, so help her focus on the areas where she is more likely to generate her bonus even though it means she has to travel away overnight for the opportunities. Is she less or more likely to go willingly and without complaint, and will she re-discover her mojo?

These are just a couple of examples that help us to understand that values can be a powerful motivator. By asking someone to do something in the right way that aligns with their values can generate stronger and more positive results. The challenge however is that if we don't have our values tattooed on our foreheads, how do you discover what they are and what matters to people? Well, quite simply, ask them. Engage in conversation with your people and ask them, "what did you do at the weekend?", "do you do a lot of that?", "that sounds amazing, please tell me more", "what did it feel like?" Employees will like you a lot if you show you are genuinely interested in them and will talk about their passion freely, if you will only ask them. As managers, we just need to communicate more effectively, so it doesn't feel contrived.

So, that deals with the values we hold dear on a personal level, but what about the values held by the business. If we accept that values include beliefs and attitudes that guide the behaviour, interaction and relationships that we have with others, how could that work in an organisation? If the organisation creates a value statement and it includes "professionalism", how would each individual member of the organisation contextualise this? What does it mean to them?

Let's hear some observations from Jim Jordan, of Jim Jordan Consultancy, a business coach, who develops and engages business people of all ages to be inspired to become great managers and leaders. In his story, he tells us about working in a large shoe manufacturer with substantial retail presence. His challenge was to align the values of the current management team with the business vision, and in doing so he created a process that achieved a much higher level of engagement.

*The question I like to consider first is "how can we engage all groups, regardless of age, to create cohesive solutions to today's challenges in the modern workplace?" The reason for asking this is that it has often been the case in organisations that a vision or the direction of a team has **already been decided** and is then **imposed** on the team in the form of targets and budgets constraints. Such factors, although the long-established currency of motivation, are not necessarily the way great results are achieved as they are rarely developed with any regard to values. Let me share a true story of how I tackled this issue differently.*

I was once asked to take over a business unit in the Republic of Ireland that had underperformed for a number of years. This region, comprising a number of retail shoe shops, was seen as "different" to their counterparts in the UK mainland. This fact alone caused the people employed within it to feel justifiably aggrieved by the reference and inference they were somehow less worthy.

My experience over the years has however developed within me a deeply-seated belief that when any group establishes a sense of cohesive identity with shared values, develops an understanding of the key components that constitute an effective team and are prepared to apply this knowledge, then they can achieve excellence. When this occurs in a team, they are more than capable of reaching exactly the same conclusions as those managers placed higher in the organisation that traditionally imposed their decisions and directions without consultation with those who would have to carry them out.

Adopting a radical approach at the time, I took all the store managers from this region off-site, away from the business for a couple of days, with the intention of creating a compelling vision for the whole organisation in both the North and South of Ireland. Only once the team bought into that, could they concentrate on their own more local issues. Now, that created a huge level of suspicion, but as I was experienced with developing teams that had achieved constantly high levels of performance, I was able to show them I could be trusted. Incidentally, "trust" was something that had not been displayed well with this team in the past and, as a consequence, my reputation for being a person who was trustworthy and would be committed to helping them excel, went a long way. I knew that if I could get this team to believe in themselves and align them with a great vision of what the future would look like, then they would want to share in my own goal, which was for this team to be the number one across UK and Ireland. I knew that it was my duty to create the necessary belief and confidence in themselves to deliver it.

*I asked my team to consider a number of factors that would make the difference between mediocrity and excellence. What would need to be the minimum level of growth they would have to deliver to achieve that outcome and what would make that result compelling to all stakeholders? Specifically, what would make our customers want to shop with us **and** rave about the experience? What would have to change to make the staff and managers love their jobs, rather than just turn up? What would their behaviours and communication look like when interacting with each other, the staff they managed and their customers? What would they need to do to retain the best talent in the business? Finally, what would the business need to look like and perform like to compel the shareholders to believe in the business, such that they continue to invest in its growth on the journey to becoming independently sustainable in the long term?*

I asked the group to brainstorm these questions and come up with as many ideas as possible, and to do so whilst suspending judgment on what had happened in the past and to try to transcend current level of thinking. I then asked them to project themselves forward and answer the questions as if they were ten years in the future. How were the attitudes of these around them now they were in the future? What had changed? The power of this approach is that, once they got going, they started to come up with fantastic solutions to many long-term challenges; but more importantly, they "owned" those ideas.

Once they had completed this part, I asked them to consider the top ten ideas that they genuinely felt they could deliver and to which they would commit to achieve. They did this and were rather pleased with themselves having completed the task.

I then asked them to go through their lists and ensure that all parties that would be affected by their implementation had been considered. Each of the commitments had to be compatible with the other stakeholders needs; these being clients, staff, management and directors, as well as those financially invested. With this in mind, the team had to adjust their commitments until all the needs of all the various stakeholders could be met. This caused much debate but, finally, a list that they felt needed to be delivered to achieve a compelling vision and roadmap for success for the business was produced. All of them then made their commitment to apply these, knowing that I would support them, hold them directly accountable to themselves and help them to challenge and hold accountable their colleagues.

It is clear to me that to have tried to impose the level of standard that the team placed upon themselves would have been impossible. It had to come from within.

In establishing the level of support they wanted from me, we determined that 20% of my role should be on helping them focus on becoming self-managing teams. This would give them the confidence and belief to achieve the high standards that they now desired. In addition, they asked for support to deliver the same exercise to their own teams locally to build commitment and customer service to the highest standard possible. By structuring my focus on the teams, rather than always fire-fighting issues, I was able to turn my attention to the supply chain and the improvement of products that were fundamentally right for the market and consumer. I also developed individual performance improvement programmes tailored to developing the leadership capabilities of individual managers.

What was the outcome you may ask? Well, after making a loss for over ten years, the company achieved profits of £3.7 million within the next two years. We opened a number of new stores and promoted, from within, key people to become Regional Managers. Unions, who had always been at odds with management and resistant to change and new ideas, became interested observers and interventions outside of annual reviews became the norm. More importantly, the team changed the way they managed others. The performance of each store in my Region escalated. Recognition as the top achievers was to follow and this status was held by them for many years to follow. I firmly believe that this team worked harder and achieved far more than they would have were traditional management practices adopted.

I have told this story many times over the years and I continue to work with business owners and corporate leaders to adopt similar practices with equally impressive results. As a Director Consultant within BNI (Business Network International®) I am currently working with business owners to adopt a similar model to create compelling and successful chapters.

A great story from Jim which shows that if you create a compelling vision, you can achieve powerful results. However, I firmly believe that you need to start with people that are at least willing to step-up. Those who have minds like concrete, i.e. "all mixed up and set solid," are a bigger challenge. Start with the right people and create some early success for the less willing to follow.

It is commonly known that the world has progressed through a number of ages, defined periods of evolution, from Stone Age to Bronze Age and so on, to the Agricultural, Industrial and Knowledge/Information Ages. As a consequence, the Knowledge Age in particular was where the knowledge and ideas held by a person gave them a human capital, which made them more valuable than someone who did not have that information in their heads. Today however, this no longer stands true as we have access to unlimited amounts of information, free of charge, via the Internet – and so the Connected Age is here. This mean the dynamics of an individual's value to an employer has altered. Now we recognise that "**Attitude**" is King.

Give me someone with the right attitude and they can be taught the skills they need and can be shown where to access the knowledge to apply that skill. In my opinion, around 15% of the value of an employee is in their knowledge and skills, meaning the remaining 85% is about their attitude. Now that is not to say that we don't need people with certain skills, of course we do; however, the opposite also applies as some people are just not capable of doing certain things. You know the people I mean, they can't do simple DIY like changing a plug but they can write a great story; no matter how many lessons they have or how often they take their test, they just cannot manage to drive a car. It isn't knowledge they lack but the bits that allow them to develop that skill just don't work the same as others. Knowledge is also something we still need as the Internet doesn't answer all questions and some of the content out there is not totally correct. So someone who "knows" information in a specialist area is critical, too. That's why I believe 85% is about attitude. Give me someone with a willing attitude any day as this means they **want** to learn and develop.

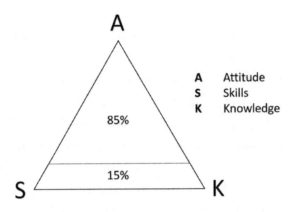

When considering an individual, a question worth asking is *"are they a can't do or a won't do?"* Give me someone who is a "can't do" and I'll give them all the time they need to help them to achieve. Conversely, give me someone who is a "won't do" means their attitude is in the wrong place as they are likely to be unwilling, and therefore resistant to your efforts and support. I hope that helps make sense?

If we accept that their attitude is driven by their values, then we need to seek employees who have a shared value with our organisation and a "can do" attitude so we can work with them on our shared and common objectives. In addition, what if we recruited people into our organisation not just around skills or knowledge but on whether they shared our values – now how amazing would that be?

"Hire attitude and train skills"
Tom Peters

The most powerful aspect of this is that, if an organisation has a particular value that is openly communicated and all the employees share in that belief about the company, then their behaviours and attitude will emulate that value at all times, and this will in turn encourage the desired culture. If we like and feel comfortable about something, then we subconsciously reinforce that behaviour. As a consequence, if a new member of staff starts work and is aligned with the organisation on day one, then strong relationships with their colleagues will be instantly formed and develop exponentially. They will be more willing to embrace the things they need to learn and, as each small success is recognised and applauded, this will reinforce positive behaviours in the right direction. Conversely, if there is a member of staff who does not share that value, then they will be incongruent with the rest of the organisation and it will be obvious through their actions. It will feel uncomfortable to them and to the people they are working with. Some tolerance will be made "because they are new", but after a while, they will either leave or be managed out.

Comparing the differences between the generations, which have developed in each through the influences they have grown up with, allows us to better understand the other. A comparative example of this would be:

Baby Boomers
o   believe that hard work will be rewarded with pay and "a fair day's

work means a fair day's wage" – work harder, earn more;

- o holding down a single career with steady promotion as a reward for hard work is seen as success, multiple jobs and careers is a rarity and loyalty is strong;
- o wealth is steadily gained and treated carefully; property ownership is an achievement but not critical as an indication of success and is part of their long-term financial security.

Generation X

- o believe their knowledge and technical competence makes them a marketable commodity;
- o they have high job expectations and, due to their knowledge, they demand quick promotion, craving feedback so they can constantly improve and will move jobs for better conditions and benefits;
- o wealth is a recognition of success giving independence and flexibility, status (perceived wealth) matters even at the cost of incurring debt to have it, home ownership is an expectation, not a goal, and is a means to create long and short-term financial freedom.

Millennials

- o believe work should challenge them but be fun, flexible and give them freedom to be creative, and knowledge is freely available so their attitude is the differentiator;
- o the workplace must align with their values (not the other way around) and they will leave if this is not the case, leadership is more important than management, and collaborating is more rewarding;
- o wealth is an expectation and instant gratification overcomes fiscal

sensibility; home ownership is beyond the reach of most and long-term financial planning almost non-existent – spending to have fun now is more important.

If we treat the first bullet point of each of the above, we can instantly see that the values and attitude towards work is different. As a construct, if we impose Baby Boomer beliefs about work on a Millennial and expect them to just get on with the job and do as they are told, and they don't, the Baby Boomer gets frustrated and enters into conflict. Conversely, the Millennial views the Baby Boomer as boring, restrictive and bossy; they respond with a poor attitude and conflict is again prevalent. If we understand the differences, then we can be more tolerant and create a workplace which plays to each of the party's strengths and values creating a win-win situation. Which would you rather have, regardless of whether you are the employer or the employee?

Chapter Thoughts and Actions:

• How can recognising the values held by an employee, help you to maximise their commitment to the business?

• What challenges might you face in dealing with a "won't do" employee?

• How will you now view "attitude" over "skills and knowledge"?

• Can you recognise the differences between the generations, but in a positive way?

Chapter 3
SO YOU THINK YOU'VE GOT POTENTIAL?

Regardless of age, race, colour, sex or creed, latest generational stereotype, whether you are currently in a management or supervisory role, or just starting out on your career path; I'll bet that you believe you are good at managing people. For those already doing it, I guarantee that if you decide to you can be much, much better by adopting some of the stuff in this book. For those who are aspiring to develop your career, this book will help you to accelerate that process, get you noticed sooner and whilst travelling on your journey of discovery, you will decide to become a great manager.

To help get you started I've told you a little about who I am, purely as a means to help you understand that this book is all about the practical application of management technique. I've also told you about how understanding a person's values can get better results. Hopefully you're starting to realise that this book is also about how experiences teach us much about how to communicate, manage and lead people more effectively. This experience, followed by reflection on what could be done better the next time, is the process of "test and measure". I urge you all to adopt this methodology and not just blindly follow everything I tell you, but rather use what I've learnt, decide to apply it, then tweak or adapt it to the particular circumstances you are faced with; but please don't lose the essence of the technique you are using.

However, despite all the knowledge you may glean from this book or other books, articles and seminars, the practical application of the management of people – employees in particular – is not necessarily easy. So, if you still want to read on, then let me explain my own personal theory about managers and hopefully whether you are a Baby Boomer, Generation X or a Millennial, you will be able to relate this to your current situation and seriously consider how you may be able to influence change. On that note, just because you are the employee not the manager, does not mean you should be unable to influence change. Just consider how you communicate the message.

It is my firm belief that many people get promoted into a position of authority by default. They didn't actually set out to be a manager and, in some cases, they didn't even think they had to be excellent at the job they were employed to do, never mind be a manager too. Quite often, their beliefs in themselves extended just far enough to allow them to do enough to get paid each month. Now does that sound familiar? All of a sudden, they are noticed by senior management for being hard-working and conscientious, and before you know it they've been promoted, which is just and right. Reward hard work, give them a raise and make them feel proud of themselves; after all, isn't that what everyone wants, including you?

Next, let's consider how the employee feels about themselves. Why didn't this happen earlier, "it's my right, I deserve it for working so hard", not forgetting that the extra money will be of use too. Does this sound like something you would say? If it is, what could you do differently to encourage your manager to notice you and want to promote you, rather than you waiting to be noticed and hoping for the best?

Unfortunately, things don't always go to plan because you may be overlooked for that promotion and someone else gets it instead. You see, quite often the employee who actually gets promoted is sometimes just in the right place at the right time and possibly doesn't have an ounce of managerial capability within them. The company had a need and "Jennifer" is the person standing in line when the decision was made. Jennifer takes the promotion because she is attracted by the status and the money, yet taking on the responsibility that comes with the role isn't what she set out to do. Once in the role, it is often a harsh awakening and she realises she isn't cut out for it in the first place. Does that sound too harsh or do you know some managers like Jennifer who are just like this? Just so you know, that is a rhetorical question!

> ## "I determine to render more and better service, each day, than I am being paid to render. Those that reach the top are the ones who are not content with doing only what is required of them."
> **Og Mandino**

Understanding why some people are good at managing and others are not will give you an advantage. What you do with that knowledge is then up to you. Allow me to share my thoughts about the different types of managers and hopefully you will see what I'm driving at.

I think you'll agree with me that there are a number of people in managerial or supervisory positions who should not be allowed to be in charge of anyone, and in some cases, they are not even fit to look after themselves! Then again, there are people who seem to easily engage with the team they work with, leading naturally, encouraging and getting the most out of them. It was through observing the behaviours of people like these from each end of the scale that made me start to ask **how** they did it. More critically, with the ones that got positive results and operated really effective teams, I wanted to know how they seemed to do it with such ease. My conclusion is simple; it is all about where on the management spectrum they lie.

The following is my distilled assessment of the many people I have met and worked with in respect of whether they can manage or not. When it comes to managerial aptitude the:

- Top 10% (91%-100%) – are "natural" managers, their ability to know the right "hot button" to press in order to motivate and encourage their staff is an instinctive thing. They intuitively know that (metaphorically speaking) there is a time and a place for motivation through alternating the use of a baseball bat or kid-gloves. It's a balance and they understand this. They get the concept behind the "Steel Fist or Velvet Glove". They appreciate employees as valuable assets that need to be handled with care, yet are prepared and competent to peel back the top of the glove and show a "bit of steel" by being firm, fair and most of all consistent. Their decision-making is decisive and is usually right. They are confident about those rare occasions when they get it wrong and welcome constructive criticism and guidance on how they can improve. They will seek additional means to increase their knowledge and people skills. Who, in your experience, do you know that fits this managerial type?

Then the next level down (and that is not meant to be derogatory) are those that are between:

- 56%-90% – these people are "good" managers, open-minded and prepared to learn how to become better at what they do. They read relevant books, articles and attend seminars to develop themselves openly, canvassing constructive criticism so they can use this to improve themselves and how they manage others. In identifying such individuals, coaching and nurturing them can reap huge befits later as they become strong motivators of employees and achieve many tangible results. Interestingly, such managers can never become "natural" but learned behaviour can get them pretty close. The positive aspect here is that good managers also fully understand the concept of the "Steel Fist or Velvet Glove" and actively look for ways to utilise this, as they are constantly striving to be better themselves as well as to get the most out of the teams and individuals they are responsible for.

I'm sure you can relate to such individuals and possibly even identify with managers like these. They constitute over 35% of managers in the workplace. Wouldn't it be amazing if we could develop more of our managers to fit into this category? I know I'd be happy to be managed by someone with this sort of attitude and skill-set.

So who's next? Well this is an interesting group as these managers (on the whole) want to be better and are formed by those between:

- 36%-55% – so these generally are "poor" or "just ok" managers, but all is not yet lost. If we support these managers with constructive coaching and encourage them personally to develop and grow, they could improve sufficiently to make it into the good manager bracket. The issue is that at the moment they just don't have the right skills, knowledge, support or attitude, or mind-set to deliver effective management. What makes the key difference is whether they are prepared to open their minds to the possibility that they could be better than they currently are AND there is a supportive organisation behind them to help them on that journey. Without that they won't make it. Those that fail on their own merits are often arrogant and do not believe they need to improve, and all they actually serve to do is make those around them miserable.

If you are the CEO of the company, or a key senior manager, it is important to recognise the signs that things are not going well. One such indicator of poor management is a high staff turnover. If lots of people are leaving (and to be perfectly honest most "exit interviews" are worthless as it is rare you get the truth from an employee who has escaped from the company) then there is usually an issue with someone in the business who they have worked with. More often than not it's the manager. If you are their manager, it is YOUR job to identify these traits and do something about it.

Alternatively, if you are the employee who is disgruntled and about to leave for another job, have you raised your concerns with anyone? How can people be expected to improve if they don't know they are doing something wrong? I don't mean complaining just for the sake of it either, you need to have reasonable justification. Poor managers are often unaware of their failings. Just for clarification – and I detest bullies – telling you off once or being curt occasionally, is not bullying; but by the same token you should not have to suffer an over-bearing work environment that makes you feel you are worthless or where you start to hate coming to work, because of how you are treated or spoken to. If you are, take control and raise your concerns; there is always a grievance process of some sort you can action.

If you are in charge of a poor manager, then you too should be taking responsibility to address issues. If nothing is done, or they are not directed to improve, then they could slip into being very poor at people management and an opportunity is lost to develop that manager to engage with their team. If they are left unsupported, then bullying of the staff is a single step away because they do not have the skill-set to be better and manage the situations they are faced with. If you are the CEO of the organisation, do you want your people to fail, or worse still have an employee leave and bring a lawsuit against your company? If not, then take action and do it now! Remember, I said earlier that it is not what we hear or say, it is what we <u>do</u> that matters – and now is the time to take action. You have a responsibility to act before it's too late!

Finally we get to the:

- bottom 35% – such people should **not** be in a managerial or supervisory role at all. Now I accept that this is a bold statement, but as a business owner or a key senior manager, do you really want your managers to be so bad that employees begin to hate coming to work? Often the reason such employees are managers is because, as Lawrence J. Peter, who developed the Peter Principle, says "managers rise to their level of incompetence". Often great and technically adept individuals are given managerial posts because "we need to give this person more and he's at the top of their pay band". However, promoting someone just to reward them is a flawed process and poor decision-making. Nevertheless, I believe there are other ways to motivate individuals through the 3 R's – recognition, reward and responsibility; more on this later – without necessarily promoting them out of their comfort zone.

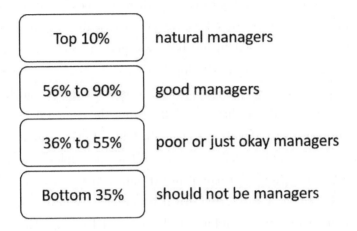

Top 10%	natural managers
56% to 90%	good managers
36% to 55%	poor or just okay managers
Bottom 35%	should not be managers

When explaining this construct, a question I have been asked is whether or not all organisations need or should have "natural managers" in their structure. The simple answer is no, but it makes the job a lot easier. As an alternative, having a business strategy that seeks to develop really good managers will help to shape your organisation into one where employees enjoy coming to work and are engaged, motivated and productive. What then does your people-strategy look like? Do you even have one? Just for the record, I don't mean your personnel or transactional HR function, I mean at Board level. This is where developing an effective and clear people-strategy will increase your staff engagement and consequently their productivity, which according to the *Dale Carnegie Institute* will be by around 25% more. In my opinion this means they will also be 25% more profitable. Now think about how that makes putting the effort compared with not doing anything and having a workforce working at half their capability!

Fortunately, dealing with those managers who are above the 35% mark is less of an issue, so long as you can identify where they are on the management spectrum. Even better would be to get them to recognise this within themselves, making sure that you have communicated the fact that you, as their manager/boss, are then willing to take action and support them to develop further.

Those below 35% are a whole different matter!

To start with, let's consider what the consequences are of not doing anything. Usually, people promoted above their level of competence are often very good "technicians". What I mean by that is they are good at the job which got them recognised in the first place, however, as soon as they are given management responsibility everything changes and there are many reasons for this:

> 1. The newly promoted manager is unable to reconcile the fact that they now have to manage employees who until a short time ago were their peers, maybe even their best friend. Being able to treat people in the workplace differently to the way they are treated socially is often an awkward transition and it can feel like an insurmountable task to have to tell someone to do something for you if they are not open to receiving the instruction. Some employees resent their friends being promoted and make life difficult and there's a great expression which sums this up – "people don't mind you getting ahead, until you get ahead of them"!

2. As a manager you automatically give up the "right to be liked" and respect has to be earned. Unfortunately, it doesn't come with the job title and employees who have earned the respect of their colleagues because they are good at doing what they do may not be good at handling the fact that they are no longer respected in the same way as previously. After all, they were good at the job before they were promoted but now they have to prove themselves as a manager. The job is totally different, and to the new manager it can feel like starting afresh.

3. The power goes to their head. Some people believe that having been promoted, this gives them a disproportionate influence and control over others. In reality it does, in respect of being able to discipline or even dismiss them; but if we accept that management is a balancing act of knowing when to take firm action or find a way to compromise, then abusing that power can have disastrous effects. Employees who resent the way they are treated by their managers can easily withdraw their discretional effort and effectively work to rule. Business needs engaged and motivated employees, not the opposite.

4. Worse still, if this power is treated by the new manager as absolute, then they may escalate their management techniques in order to bully their staff. This is a self-defeating prophesy; manage the employees badly, they work less, placing pressure upon the department to perform, resulting in the manager shouting and bullying the employees to perform better, who don't because they are disengaged and so on. The worst situation is where the manager also threatens the employees if they complain above them, then they "will

suffer", whatever that may imply. Now I hear you say that this is not possible, that managers don't treat staff in this way and that bullying is not prevalent where you work. Great if that is how it if for you, but I have witnessed through observation, as well as experiencing it first-hand, where there is a culture of blame and fear and it is hugely destructive.

5. The manager just cannot cope. They do not enjoy their new role which now comes with additional responsibility, with more admin and so many meetings. It is estimated that managers in companies with over 250 employees can spend up to fifteen hours per week in meetings that don't actually produce anything. There are unrealistic demands placed upon them by their managers to deliver reports, results, less staff turnover and more profit. They have staff performance issues to deal with, having little or no understanding of how do this effectively or with meaning (hopefully you'll be pleased that I will be discussing how to develop effective performance in a later chapter). In many cases, being so overwhelmed by the role can result in poor treatment of their subordinates and a lapse into the downward spiral of bad management and bullying. This can also manifest itself within the manager as an illness and/or work-related stress, further adding to the ineffectiveness and under-performance of their department. If HR gets involved, it's likely that the manager will leave, or be "exited", from the organisation and quite often a trail of 'skeletons in the cupboard' are discovered after they have left.

CEO: "This organisation has a blame culture!"
CFO: "Whose fault is that then?"

It then becomes easy to blame the manager who is no longer there rather than looking for ways to fix the problem. Let me explain this in a different way: if you are treating someone with a large wound on their arm, it requires first aid. The action you should take is to apply direct pressure with a bandage. If blood still comes through the bandage, then you apply another. Again if there is blood seeping through due to the severity of the wound, you apply a third. If it is still bleeding then you must take all the bandages off and look for the underlying issue, perhaps something you missed when examining the wound in the first place. To bring this analogy to business terms, blaming the manager and replacing with another similar person doesn't resolve the underlying issue which is quite simply that the manager was ill-equipped to do the job in the first place. It doesn't make good business sense to set your best people up to fail. What then can be done to change this?

To begin with, consider **not** promoting the employee in the first place. What are your reasons for giving the promotion? Is the employee hungry and asking for it or does it just suit the organisation as an easy fix? Just because an employee is exceptional at their job, i.e. a good technician, it does not necessarily follow that they are going to be a good manager of people, as this may require a different skill-set and attitude. Alternatively, is the intention to promote into the role so that the employee can be rewarded? Perhaps you feel it is the only way to give them more salary and because they are a good employee you want to make them feel valued? What happens however if they are promoted and fail, leave or get fired? This really isn't rewarding the employee but quite the opposite. Can you afford to lose good people and their contribution to the business, or even worse that they stay but demotivate others, causing them to leave? What would the real cost of that be?

We could, of course, consider a more radical approach. If you've already promoted them and it's not working, will you be bold enough to demote the employee back to their previous role? I appreciate it needs to be handled sensitively, but having done this personally over half-a-dozen times, every employee has personally thanked me and were grateful to be back in their comfort zone, even though it resulted in them taking a reduction in salary. The reason why this is often seen as too difficult is because it requires dealing with the employee's emotions, expectations and the management of their colleagues' reactions, so it is much easier to ignore it. Unfortunately, if you are their manager, you have a responsibility to tackle the issue. To add to the difficulty, apart from having had an increase in salary, the failing manager is also likely to lose face. If you've handled it badly, then that is your fault and you will be viewed by everyone in a negative light because of that.

If you believe, as I do, that money is **not** a motivator except in the short-term, then this can help you position the necessary steps in a positive way. For example: you can give someone a £5,000 pay rise, yet three months on they'll still be complaining about being broke; it's just now they are at a different level. Managing the loss of face or status, however, is much more difficult to deal with, but strong communication and an explanation of the benefits of returning to a role they are good at – without the added stress – can go a long way when discussing this with the under-performing manager. If you ignore the problem and the under-performance escalates to a severe level, then HR may be supporting you in a disciplinary process of which dismissal may be the end result. As one of the alternatives to dismissal could be to demote the employee, then it is certainly something worth thinking about as you will at least retain an employee who is good at what they do and, because you haven't fired them, will actually be more loyal. After all, if you have someone who has worked for you for ten years, they hold a lot of intellectual property and knowledge of your business – why would you want to dismiss them and lose them to a competitor, in addition to the actual cost to replace them?

Let me tell you about one such occasion where demotion was the right, and only, option.

Before I became the Operations Manager in the media business, I knew that the Manchester Office had employed a really good broadcaster; let's call him David for now. He had a great voice and was a hard worker. He was committed to the company as he'd been with us since we opened that particular base, had helped recruit new people to the team and had also helped train them. On the surface, he showed management potential and so he was promoted to manager of the office and basically left to get on with it.

To start with there appeared to be no issues and our clients, the radio stations, loved what the team in Manchester were providing. As time evolved, I gained promotion into the role of UK Operations Manager and about 15 months into his tenure, I visited Manchester on my rounds. A number of staff from his team told me they thought that David had "lost the plot" and they were concerned. The company was starting to get complaints from our clients, which had an impact on revenue. He was shouting at the staff, changing their shifts at short notice and coming to work dishevelled. I watched what was going on and then had a cup of coffee with David, as what I saw was someone bullying his team and that had to stop. In exploring what was going on, I realised that the previous management had been told David was struggling, but instead of alleviating the issue, had actually given him more work to do. He broke down and sobbed.

Apart from the pressure he was under, he had lost his house due to financial difficulties and was living in his car parking overnight at a nearby motorway service station, where he would shower about once a week and use a local laundry to do his washing. He wasn't able to cope and was considering suicide. It was obvious we had let him down and had not supported or trained him to carry out the role of manager. Worse still no one had listened to his problems, and as a consequence he was in a downward spiral and taking it out on the staff. The easy option would be to terminate his employment, but I praised him for the things he was good at, such as the broadcasting. We discussed various options and agreed to demote him back to a broadcasting role only, removing the managerial pressures. He accepted the drop in salary even though this placed him in greater financial burden, however, once the team knew what we had done, they pulled together letting him stay overnight with them free of charge. We also found him a debt management company to help him sort his finances out. David went back to being a great broadcaster and stayed with the company for many more years. The original failure by the company was two-fold: they promoted him without training or supporting him, and then failed to manage him in the role.

So let's consider what is required to equip the employee to be effective as a manager. I don't mean just send them on a course as that happens all the time and doesn't necessarily teach the skills necessary to be a good people manager. However, another much more radical and, in my opinion, more effective means of ensuring you develop strong managers, without them losing face or salary, is to place them in a non-substantive position as manager for 3 or 6 months. This allows the employee to decide if they want to be a manager, if they are any good at it, and to allow you as a business to fully support them in their development. If either side doesn't feel it's working out, then the employee goes back to their previous role; which of course must be back-filled with a non-substantive or temporary person too or it won't work. If you are the employee seeking management, would you rather be able to see if you are suited to the position and responsibility, or be thrust into a role you are ill-equipped to handle?

This is not a new concept. After all we do this with new employees when they start under a probationary period, which is about allowing the business a chance to see if they are able to do the job and for the new employee to decide if the job is right for them. Why should this be any different for a newly-promoted manager? The advantages of doing it this way are that the organisation and its employees all recognise that budding managers can express a desire to progress in the company and be allowed to try it out as an "Acting Manager". If the acting manager doesn't do their job well, or becomes over-bearing, they can be moved back to their previous role before too much damage occurs and the company doesn't lose the knowledge, skills and expertise of that employee. The acting manager also understands they can step away from the role if they don't like it, knowing with confidence that their previous role is available for them to go back to as their role is filled with someone in a temporary non-substantive role too, so it doesn't create a situation where the acting manager is stuck. This also allows the organisation to "try before they buy" by being able to assess who has potential for promotion at a later date, thus developing effective succession planning.

> ## "Too many companies believe people are interchangeable. Truly gifted people never are. They have unique talents. Such people cannot be forced into roles they are not suited for, nor should they be. Effective leaders allow great people to do the work they were born to do."
> **Warren G. Bennis**

In addition, there is no loss of face or status so long as all employees understand this is the culture of the organisation. More importantly for business effectiveness, senior management can properly assess the manager in the role they are doing, how they manage staff, how they cope with the responsibility and can provide full support and training during this time. The added advantage for the employee is that they have not had an increase in salary, so returning to the same level of remuneration does not create a financial issue for the employee. If they are successful in the role and made substantive, the salary increase can always be back-dated.

It is critical that the rules are established and adhered to along with the development of a strong supportive culture from the top to the bottom of the organisation. If there is no "buy-in", it is doomed to failure. On balance, the benefits would result in a tangible open culture and engage the workforce as everyone would see complete transparency.

CFO: "What if we invest in our people and they leave?"
CEO: "What if we don't and they stay?"

As a final point, the training and development of your managers is essential. Failing to do so should be treated as a "single point of failure!" In addition, any development must be meaningful or it is just a waste of time, money and effort. Whatever has been learnt should be discussed and seriously considered for implementation on their return to the organisation, otherwise it is just lip service. Admittedly, not everything can be taken on board, but all too often, the individual returns full of enthusiasm and ideas that could potentially help grow the business, but are instantly told to "get on with the job". Deflated, the knowledge and ideas are placed on a shelf to gather dust and the opportunity for potential change has been lost. All too often this is due to a mind-set that training is a cost not an investment. Consider the comment between a CEO and CFO where the CEO asks: "What if we invest in our people and they leave?" to which the CFO replies: "What if we don't and they stay?" In the first instance, we need to encourage the right training for all our people to get the right results in developing them, followed by knowing what the learning points would bring if implemented back in the workplace. Only then can you hope to generate a tangible return on investment (ROI) from your people.

Chapter Thoughts and Actions:

• Can you recognise where those in supervisory positions are on the management continuum?

• How will you deal with the progression and promotions of employees into management?

• How will you deal with the bottom 35%?

• If you can't improve a bad manager, consider busting them back to their previous role, don't just get rid of them as they could well be a brilliant "technician" and valuable to your business.

Chapter 4
THE TROUBLE WITH THE SYSTEM

In the United Kingdom, the expression "Human Resources" was not really in common parlance much before 1980. Until then it had always been referred to as "Personnel", and in some businesses and certainly within the mind-set of the older generation of business people, it still is. Now, we over-use the expression 'HR" and apply it everywhere, but I'm not convinced many people actually understand the difference. I still get people saying to me when I tell them what business I am in, "oh you hire and fire then?"

If only it were that simple. The HR profession can fall foul of the "hire and fire" mentality, and this is not to say that HR shouldn't recruit, select and on-board employees, but I believe this should be a specialism within that arena. For example, in my own business, I don't recruit people, but instead I work with specialists in that arena and dismissal is a last resort. Furthermore, if we take HR in general and consider its future in a modern world, then clear differentials between these two areas are essential with real HR being developed by professionals with a clear business mind-set.

> ## "If your CFO is more important than your CHRO (Chief Human Resource Officer) then you're nuts."
> **Jack Welsh**

Allow me to explain why Human Resources as a profession is often marginalised by those at the top and, what I firmly believe, is the difference between HR and Personnel. In an attempt to bury the expression 'Personnel', we have developed the phrase "Transactional HR", again without really allowing people in that profession to understand what it really means. Fundamentally, all businesses require both aspects in order to function and both are critical in any organisation, but HR is a strategic function whilst Personnel (or Transactional HR by its very name) is a transactional function.

The transactional aspect of the role requires things like forms to be produced, documentation and template letters to be created, policies written that accurately reflect the rules and processes of the organisation, contracts of employment (written, issued and checked back in to be filed), job descriptions and interviewing processes, induction packs and processes for new starts, organisation of and invitations to training programmes, and payroll. In a word: "Administration". Without it, the organisation will struggle to function, so I'm sure you'll agree it can be a large, complex and, at times, a fairly critical job role.

On the other hand, human resources operating effectively in a business should be providing a strategic focus to the organisation. There is much debate about this at present although I believe the place for HR is interacting and integrating at Board-level, challenging the CEO and Finance Director on their decisions. That requires a business mind-set, not a process-driven one.

Here's an analogy; you need more staff which is the WHAT you need, i.e. the outcome or the result. The processes for on-boarding the new staff deals with the HOW, i.e. how it is actually done. Strategically however, the question should be WHY? What I mean by this is that you need to know why you are recruiting for a new Operations Manager, and only once you have answered that question is the process you utilise to achieve this relevant. To think about the situation from a WHY perspective and challenge this, has much more meaning than just carrying out the TASK!

> **"If the main purpose of HR strategy is to create competitive advantage through people, then it implies that you have to change the way you manage those people."**
> **Paul Kearns**

So let's consider the dilemma faced when you need to recruit a new Operations Manager as the last one has just resigned, or worse still already left. Of course, you need to have an exit interview and find out why the person left, whether it was something you did, or whether he or she just got head-hunted to go to a bigger and better role, or your competitor; but for now let's not get distracted.

The easy solution and one that most HR people will adopt, is to just recruit like for like. The issue here is that any employee (never mind someone at a senior level) will not only have developed **in their role** but will also have developed **the role itself**. They will have a large amount of intellectual knowledge about the organisation, which may be lost once they leave, and many are likely to take contacts and information with them. Worse still, if they have not left amicably, there is a danger they will create issues that will only be found when they are long gone. Every time then that a person, especially someone with any standing in the organisation leaves, the question to ask is not: "who will we get to replace them?", but rather "what role, type of person, experience shall we replace them with?" You cannot replace a person who has worked in an organisation with someone who has never been there and expect them to be as good as the person that left. Instead they will bring an alternative perspective, ideas and opportunities to the company. This should be embraced, not criticised, and consultancy-focussed thinking will naturally consider whether this is an opportunity to restructure and make the organisation better rather than just filling a vacant position. It may be that the right decision is to replace like for like, but at the very least full consideration should be given regarding the impact if a different stance is taken. Ask yourself, what would the right outcome for the business look like?

In order to start considering this, a particularly relevant thought-process is required, especially considering that Millennials will constitute two thirds of the working population by 2030. Being born after 1980, they will have a much more transient attitude to the work place. Before they are 60 years of age, most will have had five different careers and at least ten jobs with different companies. This makes their transferable skills, experience, knowledge, values and – most importantly – their attitude, an essential attribute when selecting them for a role they may only commit to for a relatively short time before they move on. How then do we ensure the new "Operations Manager" is the right person and also someone that will add value to the organisation?

Peter Wisniewski, HR Director for Nike based in Sunderland, once shared with me his thoughts on this matter and showed me a diagram to better explain this:

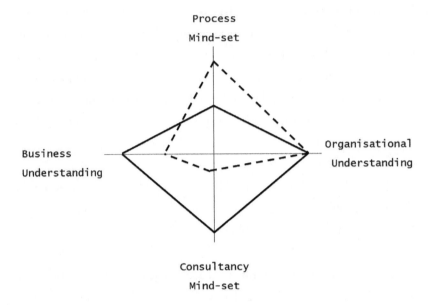

As a manager within the business seeking support from HR, would it be better to have someone who understands strategic functionality of the organisation or just the processes? The development of effective HR in an organisation requires those doing that role, or you as a manager who has to do the HR bits as part of your current job, to be effective at a strategic level. They and/or you need to be where the SOLID shape is, not the DASHED. This requires having, or developing, a balance between "Business" and "Organisational" Understanding.

In other words, you need to **know** about how business works, and not just the one you are employed in, but business in general. Make it your objective to learn about the wider world. Most HR people know all about their own organisation and its structure, where the employees exist in the company, what they do, their job descriptions, salaries, who their line managers are etc.; but how many of them can read a budget spreadsheet effectively and are therefore be able to use a common-language when discussing financial matters with the CFO? To be really effective, HR people must also develop a consultancy mind-set which is "solutions-focussed", not a general HR/Personnel mind-set which tends to be "process-focussed".

One of the other areas that HR needs to master is somewhere in between. This is the caring, welfare aspect to the role. The reason it sits between the two is an employee who is struggling with their work through illness or injury, will need to be supported through some capability process, focussed on returning them to the workplace. By its very nature it's a process, however this doesn't stop there and to treat employees as just part of a process is being unfair and uncaring. Strategically, having employees who feel valued and cared for, will not only help that employee to return to work sooner and be of value to the organisation, but the rest of the workforce will be watching how you treat that employee. They will make a decision on their own engagement and commitment, and how long they will stay, through what they observe. The balance of empathy, not sympathy, is critical and must be led by the HR department, although it is as important that the individual's line manager understands how and what to do as well.

Let me share with you a story from Nigel Morgan of Morgan PR that shows how, from his perceptive, the human resource function failed to support him properly. As you will see, the support mechanisms were left to those he worked with rather than the organisation who should have made sure it happened.

Nigel runs a successful PR company, which challenges the standard way of thinking when promoting your organisation. He attributes this to five years defending the thin blue line for a major UK police force. After leaving, he established Morgan PR, a boutique public relations and social media consultancy in 2002, specialising in case studies that truly promote and help businesses grow. He still helps the police out from time to time and is a calm influence when a crisis hits. Nigel tells us of the challenges he faced which ultimately impacted on his health and how the organisation handled that.

Being a police press officer was an exciting, daunting, 24-hour, 100 mph, roller coaster of murder and mayhem and, if you forgive mixing up emergency services, it was mostly fighting fires and keeping stuff out of the media; as much as promoting the exceptional work the boys and girls in blue delivered every day.

A promotion to a bigger region brought with it many more crises and stories that needed to be carefully worded before being shared with the wider community. It wasn't about cover-up but more about sensitivity towards the affected parties. With the increase in pressure, this started to take its toll on me, such that I was not coping working excessive hours with disrupted sleep and a total loss of any work-life balance. Although I was working considerable overtime that I was meant to take as time off in lieu and didn't, deep down, I did not believe that my benign role was surely that stressful compared with the police officers risking life and limb every day.

When I first got into journalism, it was exhilarating. I was fresh-faced, filing copy from a payphone on a tight deadline, with the editor screaming at me and the ink from the last interview still drying. Without question it was crazy, stressful and fun, topped off by the sense of achievement in always getting the story. This gave me great satisfaction. Now being a police press officer was much the same, with the main difference that I had to ensure the "thin blue line" was portrayed in a positive image as one serving the public, especially one that protected and supported victims.

However, the difficulty with the stresses of such a job are that it impacts on your home life. It wasn't helped by a complicated marriage. My wife worked away in Scotland for long periods, which made me falsely assume that I had more time to concentrate on my work. For a number of weeks, I found myself arriving at work before 6 a.m. and not leaving until eight or nine in the evening, having emailed myself files to read. Consequently, I would grab a bite to eat and work on through midnight, often catching just a few hours of sleep. I was routinely working 18 hours a day without realising I was about to hit a wall. At least I was submitting my time-sheets, which incidentally were happily signed off by HR who appeared not to notice my excessive hours.

I was well into a working week of nearly 100 hours when we had to deal with a major incident. This resulted in me appearing live on television, speaking alongside the then Prime Minister Tony Blair. High level, high stress stuff but it was what we were trained for. What I hadn't recognised was that a perilous shift in brain chemicals had been happening unnoticed during my long working hours. When I disagreed with an operational decision, which I felt compromised a victim, I marched into the control room and tore a strip off the commanding Superintendent.

I've no recollection of what I said in that room but I do remember being out of control. To the Superintendent's credit, she recognised I was in distress rather than being insubordinate, and the police service stepped up to rescue me. I was taken home, followed the next day by multiple welfare calls, which led to me being given a referral to the force's Occupational Health Practitioner. The "process" had started.

After a sleepless night, I received a phone call from Occupational Health, which was all soft-voiced and soothing, inviting me for a chat. I drove like a man possessed, taking thirty-five minutes of what should have been a one-hour journey, as at the time I believed that a single visit would solve all my concerns. I was told all about stress and how common it was and that I should not worry. It felt very transactional and lacked any depth of sincerity. I did not feel supported at all, rather that I was just part of a process, which in my state just seemed to make things worse.

Dissatisfied with how things were panning out I went to my GP who I knew quite well and she listened to what had happened. I was prescribed antidepressants and signed off for six weeks. Being in denial, I exploded and told her to 'Foxtrot Oscar', storming out in a flurry of door-slamming. To her credit, she pursued me and would spend another hour talking me off the metaphorical ledge before adding some sedatives to the mix. I was clearly a lot more unwell than I first thought, and in reality it would take me three months to get out of my deep depression, back to reasonable functionality; although even today it still affects me.

Occupational Health plugged me into some counselling and although my doctor signed me off for a further six weeks, the attitude from head office was "there's nothing really wrong with you". To HR, it was just a process and in their opinion, after the six weeks, it was time I got back to work. An assessment panel was then convened to determine what would happen to my sick pay. The advice my civilian line manager was given from HR was to halve my sick pay to "encourage me back to work". Thank goodness for the support I received from my work colleagues, both civilian and uniform, as they made me feel valued and showed genuine concern for my well-being. However, I did not feel the same about head office and HR.

The medication, counselling and unstinting support of my colleagues helped me return to work on a gradual basis and I recall spending less time in work than I did commuting that first week. The most astonishing thing was the number of senior officers who came to see me. They would quietly shut the door and then reveal their own experience of depression before giving me their personal mobile number in case I ever needed to call. It was humbling and refreshing. There was no stigma and my recovery continued. How powerful would it have been if someone from HR had been involved in those discussions? Maybe they would have been had they been considered as open, honest and approachable. In my opinion, HR didn't just fail to support me, they also failed to support my line manager and those colleagues who genuinely tried to offer me help.

Depression cost me my marriage and my job! While ultimately it has made me stronger and equipped me to help others, I would rather not have gone through that journey. What remains with me is the fact that individuals who supported me did so through their own natural desire to do so. Unfortunately, this was done with no direction from those who should have been taking on that responsibility. It's made me realise that HR should not be an isolated department just following a tick-box exercise, but something that should be interwoven throughout all levels of the organisation. In that way they could be the "experts", there to support those who need to manage their people better.

Caring for your employees and colleagues is something everyone in an organisation should do and, with the right leadership, no-one falls through the cracks.

When Nigel relayed this story to me, he explained that there were as many senior colleagues who offered support as there were those younger than him or new to the police force. The identification with a colleague in need brought out the empathy and nurturer in most people regardless of their role or experience. As a manger, or person aspiring to be one, exercising a softer tone or approach can be extremely powerful in engaging those you work with.

In reviewing this story many of you may be asking why HR was responsible and failed. In this respect I would agree. The issue here was that the automatic assumption was that HR should step in to take over the "management" of Nigel. Although his actual managers and colleagues stepped up, there was almost a feeling they shouldn't have been doing so. Herein lies the problem with HR. Where do they sit within your organisation and what role do they have? This needs defining as to whether they are transactional or strategic, in control or there as a support function. This dilemma extends to you on your management journey too. What role will you take? If you are the immediate supervisor, manager or colleague of another person, then often you are the best person to give direction and support to that individual and do not need help or support from HR or a more senior manager.

I've already told you that I joined the police service in 1984. I did so in a town called Peterlee, in the North East. At the time, I joined as a fresh-faced probationary constable; the miner strike was in full flow. My landlord, Ernie Lewis, was one of the foreman at the Easington Colliery Pit nearby. Despite the conflict, none of the miners, nor the police officers involved in the dispute were bad people. They cared about working hard and achieving the outcomes given to them. However, I don't wish to focus on those times, but rather use mining as an analogy about effective management, of which HR is a part.

From the miner's perspective, they would start the day by entering a lift that took them a mile underground and then one and a half miles horizontally outwards underneath the sea. At the coal face, there were machines for digging out the coal but also a trusty pick and shovel. Ernie was not at the coal face, but rather in the office on the surface and, as a consequence, his ability to influence what the team supervisor did at the coal face was minimal. His responsibility was to direct an overall vision and order for the day's work. The actual mining of the coal was that of the team leader – or if we apply this analogy, the line manager – and being close to the team meant they were where they needed to be to get the best results. Ernie could not have told the miner when they should use the machine, the pick or the shovel as he was too remote to the situation. It would be natural then to assume that the line manager at the coal face was competent and willing to deal with the situation. Unfortunately, this is not always the case and faced with a difficult employee issue, the manager will usually default to HR to resolve the situation. However, if HR embraces a more day-to-day functionality at the coal face, then they cannot take on a greater strategic focus from the surface without being conflicted.

The role HR should take must come from the leadership of the business, but regardless, you need to assume responsibility for dealing with the engagement of your team. You can stop using the expression when faced with an employee issue that it is, "not my problem, it's the job of HR to deal with that!" You have a responsibility to manage your team and to utilise HR to support you. To do this effectively, HR must accept they are there to support you from a solutions-focussed mind-set. If they aren't, then do something about it and lobby your line manager, explain that you can manage the day today stuff, but need guidance to help you manage the bits that are more complicated.

I remember a number of years ago, being asked by a friend of mine who had moved to the North East from Herefordshire and been newly promoted into a managerial role with the local council; his issue was he had an employee who was persistently and consistently late for work. He was becoming frustrated because he kept telling the employee to be there on time, but she ignored him and kept turning up late, creating a staffing issue with the previous shift. The HR policies on dealing with such a situation gave no leeway to him as the manager to deal with the situation beyond a conversational level with the employee. It was quite clear that HR must be involved if it required a formal disciplinary process. In this case, my friend had documented evidence, dates and times, a brief outline of the conversations, but had no power to act. As per the rules, he called the HR team at head office and asked for help. Their response was that they couldn't spare the manpower as they were too busy dealing with other more important things. As you may imagine, his view of HR dropped considerably. However, instead of being unhelpful because they were stuck in a rigid "process mind-set", they could have looked to offer some solution to the problem. For example, they could have given him the authority to act without them present and provided him with phone guidance to talk him through the situation. After all, it was a first-stage performance issue that needed dealt with, as it was not a dismissal that was being sought, just improvement.

This is where I get really frustrated with organisations which have had the opportunity to step up their HR function, but have on the whole chosen to encourage a "process mind-set", not one of a "consultancy mind-set". Over the last 40 years, businesses have changed their HR departmental structure so many times we are all starting to get dizzy. We've had HR as a centralised personnel and administration function where any problems from the front-line are passed to them and there is an immediate expectancy that, having given it to HR, the manager can regard their responsibility for the issue as having been handed over. It is no longer their problem. Wrong, wrong and wrong again! Then, we've had the decentralised world of "HR Business Partners" where organisations designate key HR people to look after a particular department or area. They become the "go to" person, being there to support the managers in handling the day-to-day employee issues. Often, they don't focus on the transactional aspect such as paperwork and discipline, meaning that doesn't get done. Instead, they prefer to do all the soft and fluffy stuff with focus groups and the like. Wrong, wrong and wrong again! This is just another means to create a situation where no one really gets to grip with the issues of managing people effectively. It becomes easy for managers to again absolve themselves of their responsibility for dealing with their people. Their stance becomes one of "I've been assigned a HR person, why can't they deal with it?" The fact that they are local instead of remote is a moot point and, in my opinion, totally irrelevant.

It would be much more effective to generate a centralised "personnel" function that handles all the transactional stuff. Then utilise HR, who after all should have exceptional people skills, to develop the managers on the front line to communicate with and manage their people more effectively. Provide them with consultancy-focussed solutions and empower them to act and take responsibility for their team. When the issue gets too complex or difficult to handle, HR should be available on-site to hold the manager's hand and teach them the most effective means to get the desired results. We learn from experience, so having been walked through one scenario, the next time the manager will be more confident about dealing with the next one. Finally, build a strong strategic-focussed people strategy at Board level that plans for the future growth of the business, communicate this throughout the organisation and then implement it!

> ## "The secret of my success is that we have gone to exceptional lengths to hire the best people in the world."
> ### Steve Jobs

If HR is to genuinely add value to an organisation it must wake up and smell the roses. HR is a strategic function. Practitioners should be business savvy, understand budgets and what EBITDA (Earnings before Interest, Tax, Deductions and Amortisation) means. They must challenge the Finance Directors/CFO's and Managing Directors/CEO's about their people strategy. If they're not doing this then they should start by challenging themselves with "why not?" Recent data suggests that in real terms, anyone above a shop floor worker who is starting a new job, will take at least 6 months of work to generate substantive revenue and value to the business.

Consider the impact of this with the Millennial Generation, who may not stay with you very long because they don't believe that the values of the organisation are aligned with their own, and therefore the organisation doesn't provide the right fit for them. What are you doing to make your business more attractive to them? Are you adjusting your mind-set to theirs or imposing how you were managed in the past? For clarification, it is not just about the company – and as a Millennial starting a new job, what was it about this company that made you want to start working for them? How are you influencing them to understand you?

I read a recent article about a large company who ran a recruitment evening to encourage potential candidates to come and work for them. They showed off their swanky offices and had drinks and nibbles at hand during the networking. However, red wine was the choice of drink, because the older management liked to drink red wine. The younger generation don't like red wine, they'd rather have a beer or water. This misunderstanding did nothing to show the candidates that the company understood them and that working for them would give them opportunities; rather, it showed that they were, in fact, out of touch. As a starting point, how long do you think those successful candidates would stay working at that company?

How much does it cost to recruit and on-board multiple employees who don't stay long enough to add that value? For many years I've said that when you add up all the costs to replace someone it can easily mount up to a year's salary. Don't believe me? These are just some of the on-costs for recruiting someone:

- Dissatisfaction of employee thinking about leaving – loss of productivity
- The removal of any discretional effort – winding down pre-exit
- Possible sabotage behaviour if employee is disgruntled and working their notice
- Cost to have on Garden Leave if not working notice
- Cost to pay notice in lieu if exited because company doesn't want them to work notice
- Cost of not having proper handover to their replacement
- Loss of Intellectual Property and Knowledge-base from organisation
- Tangible or perceived loss when this is passed to your competition
- Money paid to recruitment company to start search and selection process
- Cost to do recruitment yourself if you won't pay a recruitment consultant
- Time spent on the revision by staff of proposed CV's/resume's
- Cost of the time spent by employees to interview the shortlist – maybe even a second interview to of the final few candidates
- Possible 2 day assessment centre to make absolutely sure you get the right person

- Down time of a current staff member to support a work experience person who is being assessed
- Time to induct/orientate the new employee – on boarding – who is doing this and not doing their normal work
- Probation period where employee is engaging and learning the culture – how we do it here
- Training the new employee on the job to get them up to speed

Now how much does that mount up to? Worse still, what if the new employee turns out to be unsuitable and you get rid of them and start all over again, or what if they employee decides not to stay very long. I'm sure you are thinking that's not how it happens in my business, but perhaps you need to think again.

So, what if you had effective HR, who worked with the CEO and CFO to develop a strong employee retention strategy which kept the best people engaged and happy. What would your organisation look like if it had a strategy for developing key skills, creating an environment that provided meaningful work, offered challenges, career progression and rewarded employees properly? What about succession planning – and yes, even for a small business this has validity. Perhaps then you would be attractive to those Millennials and retain the right people in the business. Would having the right people in the right place at the right time be a much more effective support to the leadership of the organisation, generating real value and return on investment (ROI)?

Were this to occur, would HR really add value and is it more likely to have a voice in the business worth listening to?

Chapter Thoughts and Actions:

• Review where HR sits in your organisation and question whether it adds value?

• Can you influence HR Strategy and if it doesn't add value how will you enhance this?

• What aspect of the day-to-day HR role can you do rather than passing the buck?

• How much is losing good employees actually costing your organisation – is there a better way?

Chapter 5
DEVELOPING YOUR MANAGEMENT TOOL-KIT?

In a brave new world, HR should not be there to pay you, the manager, lip-service or to do your every bidding as soon as you get some attitude from one of your employees. So what are you going to do about it then?

My advice to you is that if you want to get better, then you need to develop a toolbox of techniques, things that can help you deal with employee issues. As with any good tradesmen, their toolbox becomes an extension of themselves to be drawn upon as and when needed, and is used by them instinctively. They know what works best for the given situation they are faced with. As an effective manager (which is after all your "trade"), you will utilise one or more of the tools in your toolbox as an extension of how you manage people, and only then you will intuitively use the best tool (method) to get the best outcome. Your role as manager is to get the best out of your people, and where you have an issue, you need to use the right tool to elicit a win-win situation.

This is as relevant to those who are already managers with some tried and tested methods as it is to someone just starting out on that journey. In fact, if you are that new young person seeking to accelerate your career, developing methodologies that will help you to get the best out of others is essential. The ability to connect and communicate with people, motivate and engage them, regardless of whether they are your peers or line managers, will differentiate you from those around you who just talk about becoming a manager. You have to walk the walk, not just talk about it, and to learn, you have to make a few mistakes on the way.

"No one cares how much you know, until they know how much you care."
Anonymous

In choosing the right tool, this could range from advice and guidance to the employee, placing them on a performance development plan to help them improve, or it may be severe enough to require a disciplinary process. Sometimes it will be a "cup of tea and sympathy", as employees do not always share what's going on at home even if it is impacting on their work. To be effective, dealing with issues early and not letting them fester will more often avoid the situation going awry. Remember, "no one cares how much you know until they know how much you care", so pick your moment to show some empathy and engage your team to work better for you. Allow me to share an example of what I mean.

When I joined the corporate world in 1996, I managed a team of radio broadcasters delivering traffic, travel, weather and news information "on air" in real-time. This was very fast-paced environment and getting information about a road closure or accident out to those listeners in their cars at drive-time could have a surprising impact, especially if it was wrong! Our editorial team collated information from multiple sources such as from public information lines, emergency services, electronic data and visual sightings from our "eye in the sky reporter" (helicopters and fixed-wing aircraft) flying above the nation's roads, make sense of it all and then pass it to the presenters on the ground or in the air who then broadcast this live on local and National radio stations.

The ground-anchor would co-ordinate the mike, codec and adverts (from which we made our revenue as these adverts were in a prime slot to a captive audience) and had to carry out a sequence of knob-turning, key pressing, mouse clicking and speech to get a coordinated succinct bulletin on air at the right time. With a narrow window of time, up to four times an hour, missing a bulletin and its advert could be costly, not to mention the annoyed driver stuck in a traffic jam on their way to an important meeting.

So back to the issue at hand. In the late 90's, I employed a female presenter (we'll call her Felicity – not her real name) with a great voice, good articulation and well-liked by the radio stations she broadcast to. However, she didn't cope too well under pressure. When she broadcast in the middle of the day with one or two bulletins to one or two radio stations per hour that was easy. Doing the same job in drive-time, where she had to manage four radio stations in very tight windows and to deliver three to four bulletins to each, every hour – added to which she had to present, coordinate an advert and link to a presenter in a plane – then that was a whole different issue. The problem was simple; she couldn't cope. Worse still when she made a mistake and failed to fire the advert, or turn up the audio on the plane so nothing was heard, or talked over the presenter at the radio station, she always blamed it on the equipment. Dealing with this issue was imperative. The radio station programmers were sensitive and critical, and in a fit of pique could reject the business contract in an instant. However, dealing with this problem would not have worked by shouting or pressurising her into getting better.

As a manager, you have to understand your people: what makes them tick, how they think, and most importantly what "hot buttons" to press. So get good at this before anything else. I called Felicity into my office and asked her what the problem was. Her immediate response was to fall back on her excuses that the equipment was faulty. I told her I understood and asked how I could help with that. This completely threw her as she expected to get told off and criticised for not doing her job, but I knew Felicity and that if I did this, she would dig her heels in and be stubborn. I also knew she was more capable of doing her job than she had been, and that something else was going on. Be aware, most employees won't share their personal life in the office choosing instead to let their performance suffer.

By being empathetic and showing I cared about what was going wrong and not telling her off, she opened up. She admitted without prompting that her mother was ill and she was worried about a looming hospital operation. Once Felicity told me this I was able to create some flexibility around her shifts to allow her to help with her mother. I also buddied her up with another experienced broadcaster, worked her through some intensive training and developed a list of operating processes for her to work to. If she focussed on these in order then she wouldn't miss any steps and the bulletin would run seamlessly. The simple rule here was to choose the right means to generate a win-win situation. Felicity appreciated what I had done for her and continued to be one of my best presenters for many years. Had I forced a disciplinary or performance process on her, she would have continued to get worse, and apart from risking the relationship with the radio stations, I would have lost a valuable employee.

On the other hand, I'm not suggesting that you should take this stance with every situation. In fact, the art of knowing what to say, how to say it and when to do so, is the real "black arts" of managing people.

Let me give you another means to utilise an effective tool from your tool-kit. Spencer Johnson & Ken Blanchard in their excellent book "*The One Minute Manager*" discuss how to give someone praise that motivates them and keeps them giving more. They also recommend that you take around a minute to do this effectively and that this is an excellent technique. I, however, believe that the impact is just as good if you do this in around 7 seconds. Note however that the three critical factors are that:

1. You do it immediately;
2. You must be specific about what they did; and
3. You deliver it to the employee sincerely.

The basis of a 7-second praising is to "catch someone doing something right". This is contrary to how managers are usually perceived, which is to tell people off. However, the simple act of "catching" someone being kind to a work colleague, or going the extra distance to help a customer, or even just handling a call with great customer service, is hugely powerful if you praise the employee straight away for doing it.

Here's a specific example of how this might work. You approach Alyson and say, "I just overheard you on that call to Mr Phillips. They are a valuable customer to us and I was extremely impressed at how you handled the complaint. How was he with you?" This generates a sense of pride and energy in the employee and, as a consequence, Alyson will strive to do more of the same. An additional benefit is that you are engaging with her in easy conversation, which shows you are interested in what is going on in your team and makes you far more approachable.

"Catch people doing something right and tell them right away."
Spencer Johnson & Ken Blanchard

There are many different tools that you can build into your toolbox, but be cautious once you've developed these as picking the wrong tool could create more problems than it solves. I'm sure you know someone that would rather use a hammer to put a screw into a wall. It's not really what it's meant for despite the fact that it may work in the short term. Making the best choice will come through experience, so look for different ways to manage and try to use the right tool at the right time.

Imagine just for a minute that you are a craftsman, a carpenter perhaps, brilliant with your hands and capable of achieving great things. You understand wood and how to get the best out of it, instinctively knowing which way the grain needs to be shaped to ensure it has both strength and beauty. The items that you craft are useful and long-lasting. This skill was not learned overnight and took hours of time and concentrated effort to learn how to do without thinking. It is said that to master anything at all takes 10,000 hours of consistent and dedicated practice. Fortunately, I'm not suggesting that becoming a good manager is going to take you that long, but it doesn't usually happen overnight.

I expect you are wondering where I'm going with this, but think about it just for a moment – does that not sound a lot like a manager? Someone who knows how to craft his team into something useful and long-lasting, where they add value to the company for whom they work. Now what do you think is the thing that both a good craftsman and a good manager has with them all the time? Well, quite simply, it's their toolbox.

For the carpenter – it is the chisels, mallet, sharpened saw, hammer, brace and bit, bench saw, router and so on; regardless of the actual tools, they will all be kept in his nearby toolbox. The key here is that the experienced carpenter did not buy all the tools he may need in one single visit to the DIY superstore – quite the opposite. The tools of his trade were collected over time, some tried and discarded, some lovingly kept for years because they work and just feel right when being used. From a manager's perspective, it is no different. The tools in the toolbox are just techniques rather than something physical. The expression "knowing when to use a baseball bat or a pair of kid gloves" is not literal but rhetorical, and refers to the times when you need to be strong with an employee to achieve results, and when you need to pile on the empathy to show how much you care.

In reality, there are thousands of management books, hours of video and webinars and endless seminars you can attend to "gain new insights", but like the carpenter the best way to grow your toolbox is through experience. As the carpenter would perfect his trade over time, a good manager will be constantly looking to develop theirs too. This may be in trying out a particular methodology with a difficult employee. If it works, this acts as a reinforcement and the manager will try it again the next time given a similar situation, fine tuning their craft, just like the carpenter becomes familiar with his chisel and mallet. If it is a disaster, then that particular tool may be discarded and not used again with that particular type of wood.

We are now going to hear a story from Phil Berg about some of the powerful tools that he developed for his own toolkit throughout his life. Phil Berg is the BNI Assistant National Director for UK & Ireland and Executive Director for BNI London East and Buckinghamshire. He is an internationally acclaimed Networking Expert, Motivational Speaker, and owner of "Reach YOUR Goals" where he shares many of the golden nuggets he has learnt over time to help people help themselves develop and grow.

Phil has spent most of his working life testing and trying different ways to get the best out of people. His favourite phrase about his journey is,

"I wish I knew then, what I know now!"

Being very sporty as a young man, my ambition was always to become a professional footballer. At one stage, I truly believed this would be my destiny. As a schoolboy, I trained at Tottenham Hotspur, followed by a brief period at Queens Park Rangers. Unfortunately, I came up short and didn't quite make the grade. At this stage, I feel it appropriate to make my first point about management;

*I truly thought I was good enough, **but unfortunately, the people making the decisions (the managers) "didn't".***

This negative experience completely influenced my thought process and it was at this moment I chose that, sooner rather than

later, I will be in control of the journey to my own destination.

My background is in retail sales. I spent 32 years in the carpet and flooring industry. From a standing start of just little old me, with no clients, no sales and therefore no profit, I grew the business (and myself personally) into a position where we were acquired by a large Interior Design company during 2007. At that stage, we had 23 full time staff, retail outlets and a healthy, profitable business.

So, from this position, as someone who has had to learn to effectively deal with people, I would like to share some information with you (based on my many years of management experience) on how you can become an even better manager of people and yourself. In no particular order:

Understand how to be good at managing people
*Firstly you need to understand the difference between being a **manager** as against being a **leader** and thank you to my amazing son, James Berg, for helping me on my own continuing journey with this subject. Fundamentally, the main difference is that leaders have people follow their vision and goals, while managers have people who work for them to achieve the vision and goals. Now successful business owners need to be both a strong leader and an effective manager, if they are serious about motivating their team so they will follow them in achieving the overriding objectives and business success.*

Simple techniques that can help would be:

- *Understand the different styles of the people you are managing. If people have different styles, then the person that delivers the message needs to adapt, not the other way around. We can all benefit from being much better at communicating messages and instructions, and we should do this from the stance that we need to be understood not just heard. It's not what you said to me, or what you think you did to me, it's what's I heard or what I think you did to me, that is the reality.*

- *On the communication front, talk to your people and ascertain "how" they like to be managed, accepting that you may not always be able to facilitate this, but do they like to be communicated with by email, text, Skype or formally in writing? What frequency works best – once a day, a week, a month? Face to face communication is always the best especially if you are dealing with a challenging or sensitive issue. A big "no no" however, is holding conversations by email as they can and often go terribly wrong. If you cannot meet face to face, then pick up the phone!*

- *Diarise meetings, in fact diarise everything, and do so months in advance. Let everyone know what you are doing and where you are going to be. It stops confusion and uncertainty. I myself diarise my whole diary, 12 months in advance, even when I intend to get to the gym or play golf.*

- *Employ the right people to start with Recruitment is painful, it is time-consuming and if you get it wrong, it costs you in time effort and money to do it all again. So when you are sitting interviewing, go with your gut feelings as they will generally be correct. Even if the candidate is really well-qualified for the job, you need to be questioning yourself:*

- *Will they fit in with your current team's personalities and the current company culture? Look for good people who are aligned with your values and culture, it will make their transition into your business a lot easier and they will become more effective, much more quickly.*

- *If this person who says they want to work for you gets the role, how will this affect the current team dynamics? It will change things as every new person in a team always does, but the goal should be for an improvement in the way things are not the opposite, so think carefully about this one.*

- *Is the person coachable? This is a big, big, big one for me as a person who is a "can't do" can be coached to do the job well. A person who is a "won't do" has the wrong attitude to start with, thinks they know better and is usually guaranteed to be a problem from day one.*

- *Hire slow, fire fast! If they are not good enough, provided you are sure of that and you have given them support to help them prove you wrong, then DO NOT KEEP THEM ON! You might have a challenge for a while to get them replaced, but that has to be better than your current situation in that they keep working for you!*

- *Do they match your ambition and/or expectations? Do you match theirs? One of the biggest failings in recruiting people is that the question of what is expected of both parties is not discussed, creating an immediate mismatch of what one thinks the other should be doing. Ascertain the desires, ambitions and motives of the people you are managing and do it straight away.*

- *Do you like them as a person? Is that imperative? No of course not, but it is really had to give an individual your best efforts if you dislike them and it can become really testing in those challenging moments or periods that are an inevitable part of growing your business.*

Retain the right people for the right job

My one real regret in management, apart from the fact that I didn't know then what I know now, is the day that I fired a really great guy. Looking back now I should never have fired him, but I did and that is because at the time, I hadn't worked out why I should keep him!

I used to think that everyone should be decent "all-rounders", after all, I was. This attribute and attitude was essential, particularly as the company was still a SME and because of this, my view was that we should all muck in and help out in every area. Big lesson learnt here, that is not the case! To put this into a sporting analogy, you wouldn't expect your goalkeeper to continually run up the field to score goals at the other end would you? The expression "horses for courses" comes to mind as well.

So let me tell you about this gentleman, let's call him Martin (which is a good idea, because that is his real name). Martin was and is, one of the nicest men you would ever wish to meet. Our clients loved him. The rest of our team loved him. I loved him. So why did I fire him?

Good question: It was simply because he didn't bring in enough "new" business. Instead of focussing on Martin's strengths and maximising our opportunities in those areas, I focussed on his "lesser strengths" and in this respect I'd like to ask why we use the term "weaknesses" as this is far too negative surely? So, back to Martin. What I should have done is focussed on getting new business and allowing Martin to be the person responsible for overseeing the client receiving the best support ever.

The moral of this particular story is that when you re-evaluate your current team, ask yourself the following two questions:

1) *Do you want them on your bus?*
Now in Martin's case, that was a definite "yes", so why did I thrown him off at the next stop?
2) *What seat should they be sitting on?*
It's no good letting the driver sit at the back of the bus and from Martin's perspective, I clearly had him on the wrong seat!

Learn how to motivate and keep your people motivated

- *The Golden Rule we were always taught was that we should "Treat people like YOU would like to be treated". That way you get what you want from them. However, I would suggest that the most effective way to get the best from people is to actually take this one step further and "Treat people like THEY like to be treated". That way, they will react and resonate with you far better.*

- *Get the people you manage to "own" the decisions that you ideally want them to act upon. By challenging them to think in a particular direction means that they will come up with YOUR idea, and want to implement it because they think it's theirs.*
- *The most effective way is to "Question" rather than "Tell". Say things like "What do you suggest WE do?" or "Do YOU think it would be a good idea if we did this?"*
- *Ultimately decisions have to be made by the Manager, but being inclusive with the team in those decisions will create bigger and faster "buy-in" from them. The below options are different ways to manage people but I have found that number 3 usually works best:*
  1) *I need to **let you know** what we are going to do*
  2) *Let's discuss **and I'll decide** what we are going to do*
  3) *Let's discuss **and we'll decide** which is the best way*

- *Always explain "the why" and "the benefits" to your team. By doing so and giving them the bigger picture that "the company will therefore benefit in this way if x or y is achieved", will make them feel much more inclusive with the direction the company is taking.*

- *Set realistic and achievable goals with your team, individually and collectively. Get their agreement to these, don't just impose them, and most importantly agree the "completion" dates of those goals. Finally, hold them accountable through a constant and regular review of the goal and offer support and help where needed.*

- *Be interested in them as people and canvass their ideas and suggestions on how to make the job better. Ask them frequently if there is anything else you could be doing for them. If they feel you are interested in them first, and that you value their comments and input, they will be more motivated to help you achieve your goals.*

- *Recognition is very powerful and you should look for opportunities to do this wherever possible. Finding out about their personal interests allows you to focus recognition to something that matters to them. Do not look for ways to publicly embarrass people, it's the fastest way to alienate yourself and to demotivate an individual. Always work on the principle of "praise in public and criticise in private".*

The above is a very short list that, if used will give you great foundation, to become an even better manager. I hope you have found these useful and that they can help you to make a real difference to you, your businesses and, most importantly, your family.

Do you know what? That's fine too as certain methods (or tools) work for some people and don't for others. One size does not fit all. I believe it is actually one of the problems with prescriptive management training that fails to consider the individuals or their experiences. It's why I wrote this book, as I'm dismayed every time I see an employee leave a management development course full of great ideas, tips and techniques, eager to give them a try, but they don't actually come away with anything they can try out back at base.

Those who deliver such training often give the delegates so much stuff that would change the whole company if applied. In my experience that doesn't work. There are two main reasons; firstly, to make such major changes requires a much higher level of buy-in from senior management and in some cases the Executive Board; and secondly, on returning form the aforesaid course full of enthusiasm and ideas, the delegate is told to get back to work as they've been away for a week and work is building up. It would be far more effective to give them one small technique, perhaps just a methodology to alter the language to use with a difficult employee. What if you had a series of these small changes you could apply over time that would subtly change the perception of your team of you? Would applying the scale of incremental changes encourage greater engagement? Let me give you an example:

On a recent training course, I delivered to a group of Veterinary Practice Managers, I was asked by one of the delegates how to deal with a problem with their office staff. Her staff were disengaged, displayed difficult behaviours and would not take on board changes that she and the management team wanted applied to make everyone's job easier. She told me that it seemed like a constant battle of wits between "them and us". Now, the route of the issue was that every time this lady (I'll call her Becky) had something to tell the staff, she would politely say "can I see you in my office for five minutes please?" You may think that this is a perfectly reasonable statement to make, however it did not achieve anything but hostility and certainly didn't create an environment that facilitated the changes the Board wanted to see happen. Yet what she said was not necessarily wrong, it was just the way in which it was said.

I found out that on her last management course, Becky had learnt about:

being direct; to deal with issues straight away; to be open and straight-talking. All of these are fantastic techniques, but lacked context. So instead of explaining how other managers might deal with the problem, I made sure she went away with an understanding of WHY she needed to reframe the question and a technique of HOW to do it, with a focus on the context of the people she was dealing with. She was the person at the coal face; the one who knew their personalities, their hot buttons and what got them fired up. I again reiterate here that one size does not fit all, but Becky now went away with some learning points and key techniques (or tools) that she was able to add to her toolbox and apply back in her workplace. To finish this particular story, all Becky needed to do was simply re-frame the question, relative to the people she was dealing with. It may sound simple, but Becky just needed to ask the same question in a different way.

She went back to work, and when asked by the Board to deliver a message to her team, she asked "when you have a minute, can we get together as I've something to tell you which will make your job a lot easier?" The staff, sensing some potential benefit, and more importantly being asked not told, sat down and listened to what Becky had to say. She then asked them for their comments, whether they thought this would work or not, and could they help her to implement the change. This appealed to their basic human instinct to help others and they felt involved. Fundamentally, they had been resistant because Becky had been telling them, not asking them. The result was a happier, more engaged workforce that felt their views were being listened to and who were now willing to implement changes that made their work more efficient. We can win the battle, or lose it and win the war instead, but it's your choice.

> "Good management is the art of making problems so interesting and their solutions so constructive that everyone wants to get to work and deal with them."
>
> Paul Hawken

So what do you have in your management tool kit? As an experienced manager, you have probably got many things you use to get the best out of your people. Great – but never be afraid to learn and try out something new as you may just surprise yourself. Perhaps you are a new manager or not yet on the first rung of the ladder but feel you are just starting on the journey and are eager to try out new things. That's fantastic, but take it steady, applying what you are learning little by little. Assess what works for you. We are all different and what works for one might not work for another. Build up the different tools in your tool-kit, it takes time and remember not to over-use any single tool.

Here's another example of what I mean. There is a technique for chastising a member of staff without completely demotivating them, which is called the "sandwich" technique. Faced with an employee who has done something wrong and who needs to be brought to task, the manager calls them into their office and the situation plays out like this:

> *"Hey Bill, thanks for coming in. I wanted to tell you how marvellous you were handling that difficult customer on Tuesday, you really pulled that out of the hat and they went away happy. I was really impressed at your communication skills. However, on a downside I was less than impressed with how you spoke to*

Jennifer in the staff room at the Wednesday morning tea break. She is new here and you badly criticised her even though she is just learning. Now I know that was a one-off because it was out of character for you. You have some great people skills as we've seen with how you handled that customer complaint and I'm sure I can rely on you to set a great example to the rest of the team from now on. What do you think?"

So Bill has been sandwiched! He had no real choice but to attend the meeting with his manager but at the meeting has been praised, then told off, followed by some more positive messaging. This is a great and effective methodology explained in much greater detail in Ken Blanchard's book *"The One Minute Manager"* and should absolutely be in your toolbox, but a word of caution – don't over-use it. If your staff always know that this is the only technique you are going to use when one of them needs to be given some guidance and advice, then they will come in, receive the praise, switch off during the chastisement and then listen to the praise at the end. It's a bit like straightening out a paper clip and bending it back on itself a few times, eventually it breaks and becomes useless.

Chapter Thoughts and Actions:

• Develop your techniques for managing people over time – you can't do it all at once and being really good at something takes practice.

• Try out various methodologies so you don't always apply the same techniques and be prepared to discard something that doesn't work for you.

• Do you even have a management tool-kit and if you do, what techniques will you use to build this up?

• What are you going to do to develop your knowledge, as without doing so how will you ever learn how to get better at managing people?

Chapter 6
WHAT DO YOU MEAN, DELEGATE?

Why is it that when you speak to people, especially managers, they tell you that they are great at delegating, when in reality the fact couldn't be further from the truth? Most people are hopeless at delegating. Allow me to explain in more detail:

The expression "I'm good at delegating" is usually interpreted by that person as "I'm good at passing things to other people, especially if I'm the boss!" and to clarify; just because they get the job done by someone else does not mean they are good at delegating. The *Dale Carnegie Institute* once explained this to me in detail and have a brilliant 10-step process for achieving effective productivity, particularly if you have a project to complete. Now I'm not going to go into this now, but it is well worth speaking to them if you need to develop your key staff for a large project.

"The inability to delegate is one of the biggest problems I see with managers at all levels."
Eli Broad

Furthermore, when it comes to managing projects on time, Brian Tracy in his book *"Time Power"* emphasises delegation as an effective way to maximise time management of your people. So what I'd like to do is to give you an insight into my understanding of delegation and how you might apply this simply in the management of people you have responsibility for. To start with, I feel it important to emphasise that the purpose of delegation is to get a task or project completed correctly, by someone else, within a relevant time-frame.

So, when considering delegation, there are in my opinion four factors or ways that make for effective or non-effective delegation, which I think of as the "A" to "D" of Delegation. The first three are ineffective but on the surface may look like effective delegation, so beware!

A	Acceptance
B	Binning It
C	Circulating
D	Delegation

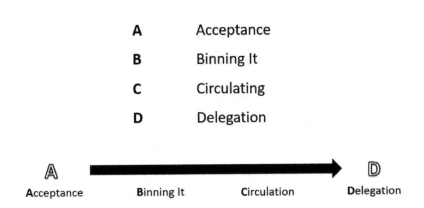

Ⓐ			**Ⓓ**
Acceptance	Binning It	Circulation	Delegation

Acceptance:

This is the first indication that a manager is unable to effectively delegate. Quite simply this is where the manager fails to delegate at all and accepts the fact that they will do the work themselves. Sometimes this can be after an attempt to delegate the task to an employee, but that person passes the ball back to the manager who carries out the task, thus avoiding the need to do it in the first place.

Ken Blanchard in his book *"The One Minute Manager Meets the Monkey"* describes this brilliantly. It may be that the manager has not even tried to delegate the task, but just decides to do it themselves. The usual self-talk is, "it'll be quicker for me to do it myself than to explain it to Fred". Worse still, having passed the work to someone else, when they fail to complete it, the manager takes it back, which just adds to the managers' workload and frees up the employee to go home early!

Being a manager is about getting work done effectively by the team you are responsible for, otherwise why bother employing them in the first place!

Binning It:

There's an interesting myth that the best way to handle the pile of papers in your "IN" tray is to just deal with the top couple of centimetres, because if you leave the rest for long enough it won't be important anymore and can be discarded – now wouldn't that make our lives easier? That is a great idea, right until the discarded document happens to be the most critical one for your business. Now, if all you want to do is to concentrate on the most important things and time is scarce, then looking back over 12-month-old out-of-date articles is not a good use of your time, so being effective in dealing with what matters is definitely the way to go. However, ignoring things is not!

So, let's think about this in a different way. Most specific tasks will have a time-frame during which they need to be done. After a while, the need for that specific task to be completed becomes superseded by other more important, relevant and time-critical tasks. Things occur in the business that distract from the original objectives and goals. For a manager who doesn't like delegating, and is prepared to keep fobbing-off requests for updates on how the project or task is going, they could hold onto the task and wait for it to be forgotten about.

When this happens, the manager forms the mistaken belief, even though it could be critical and vital, that the task is no longer necessary. With this attitude, it is obvious that the task can be dumped in the bin, allowing everyone else (including the manager) to just get on with what is now considered to be the next most important and time-sensitive issue.

In reality, actions affecting one area of the business usually have an effect on another part. The failure to deal with the task at hand often creates bigger and more difficult issue later.

Circulating:

This is the manager who doesn't delegate effectively but instead just hands out tasks for others to complete. Sometimes this may be sharing the workload out equally or it may be just giving it to whoever happens to be available at the time. What also happens is that, where the Team Leader is busy, they follow the managers' example and they just pass the task on to someone else, regardless of whether it's another manager or a member of their team. This can continue for some time with the task or project being circulated around the business. In extreme cases, it could even come back to the manager who originally handed it out and his response at that stage may be to apply A or B to the task or set it going round and round again! More importantly the issue is really about having a lack of focus with little or no accountability. However, such behaviour can often be seen by many managers as a sign of them being a good delegator. After all, if the tasks are allocated and then chased up at a later date by the manager, there should be no reason why they wouldn't be completed; except of course when it is treated by the delegated individual, who passes it on to someone else because they were not effectively delegated to in the first place!

The main problem with this approach is it rarely gives any consideration to who is the recipient of the task or project. It is just distributed or handed out to someone – anyone – who cares!

"No person will make a great business who wants to do it all himself or get all the credit."
Andrew Carnegie

So before we get into what good delegation actually looks like, let's hear a story from Russell Sawdon, who is the Co-Executive Director for BNI Durham & Teesside. Russ, along with his wife Gill, has to know how to delegate effectively to his team of twenty Director Consultants and Ambassadors to support the 400-strong member region, who by the end of 2016 were sharing £19.6 million in referred business amongst themselves. However, his ability to delegate was learned at an earlier time when he was a successful manager at a large retail DIY store, and career progression depended on how well you managed your teams;

When I managed a large retail shed for a major DIY retailer you could not survive without being a master of delegation. With a turnover of over £20M and hundreds of staff, it was imperative that you empowered people to do the things that they were great at doing.

My view on delegation is quite a strong one in that has a longer-term impact than just getting tasks completed by your employees. Without delegation, I believe we are unable to find the genuine leaders of tomorrow and, because we don't play our part properly, we don't recognise particular skills and attributes and consequently fail in our objective to develop and train people effectively.

To highlight this point, I would like to share a real story from that period of my life. Once a year, as we approached the busy Easter trading period the company ran a "Store Standards" competition with a large prize for the store if you were the highest-rated store in the country. This story relates the particular management styles of two managers, let us call them Mark and John. Mark was a control freak and as such "owned" the list of tasks that would be scored against in order to win the competition. He believed he knew every step that needed to be done and in what order to win. He also had the same management team that he had worked with for 5 years where no one had moved on or moved up. His belief was that he knew his team inside-out, what motivated them and that they were immensely loyal to him. So, this sounds like a good start with a tight team who know how everything worked, right?

Mark's methodology was to "circulate" the tasks that needed to be completed to his heads of departments and then to carry on with his own tasks for the rest of the working week. What he didn't realise was that in reality, the heads of departments didn't have any ownership of these or accountability and they subsequently passed them on again and again to other employees in their own respective teams. They did so without any checks or measures and without proper delegation, which meant the employees didn't take ownership of the tasks either. When Mark finally realised how few of the tasks had actually been completed, it was

STEEL FIST OR VELVET GLOVE

the day of the judging and it was too late to get them finished. Mark had not checked on progress, empowered his people to take responsibility, nor explained the "Why" to the team. As they had been working for Mark for so long, they were used to his style of management and knew that there were no consequences or likely rewards for doing or not doing the tasks assigned.

John on the other hand understood how to motivate people. He continually developed his team and was the 'go to' guy for career development. Several of the store managers around the region had worked with John over the past five years and gained promotion through doing so. He rarely had anyone in his store for more than 18 months. Behaviour begets behaviour and the managers who had moved on applied the style of management that John displayed, attributing to their own success.

Back to the competition, where John's methodology was to split the list of tasks that needed completing into chunks. He then shared these out among his heads of departments who were competing with each other to get the highest scores, knowing that there were some rewards for them and their teams, if they succeeded. They also knew that if just one of them let the team down that they all failed and this was not an option! John created a strong 'why' and then checked in with them all regularly on how they were doing in order to deliver their section and in what timescale. He offered guidance and additional resources for any of those heads of departments if they needed it or asked for it. This was not imposed but formed more a discussion about how to achieve the end result. As a consequence of being delegated to effectively and trusted to carry out those duties, they all succeeded and won the competition.

It was no surprise then that John was always less stressed than Mark and eventually gained promotion to a regional role, where he continued to show strong leadership, delegating effectively to further achieve higher results.

Have you ever heard the quote "If you want something doing, give it to a busy person"? People like John are always busy as are people like Mark. The difference is that Mark always focussed on his own tasks, believing he had delegated properly and as a consequence he failed to track these or follow up effectively. John, on the other hand, did his own tasks, but still checked in with those he had delegated to ensure they were being completed.

A powerful story from Russell, which demonstrates how to effectively delegate and the results that can be achieved from doing so. What then is effective delegation?

Delegation:
In order to be effective and ensure results, a number of things need to take place.

1. The person who will delegate the task or project needs to have ownership of the task, as they are ultimately responsible for seeing the job gets completed.
2. Then they need to decide who will be delegated: the responsibility to see the job to completion. Is this a single person or many, in which case each must be able to fulfil point 3 below.

3. Before delegating the task or project, the people involved are required to fulfil some criteria:

    a. Are they the right person regarding their attitude, skills and knowledge? If not, is this something they can learn? If they don't have these attributes, are they still the best person to carry out and complete the task or project?

    b. Do they have the time to do the work? If not, can they stop what they are doing or delegate other tasks to other people to free themselves up?

4. If the above are fulfilled, then the person can be delegated to. This is best carried out face-to-face, as conveying passion, vision and importance sufficiently well enough is not easy by email.

5. The task or project objectives should be discussed in detail with agreement between both parties on how it is to be carried out.

6. Finally, and this is the most critical aspect of delegation, milestones must be set at the first meeting of when progress of each completed stage will be reported back. This is necessary to hold all parties accountable and to continually reassess where the project is at presently. It also gives an opportunity to discuss where there are any issues such as whether the project deadline or milestones need to be adjusted and if additional or different resources are needed to see the job to completion.

Once finished, all parties should debrief and discuss what went well, what didn't work and how it could be improved. By doing this, any mistakes can be learnt from for the next project, but importantly, this final aspect of the role gains proper accountability and effective delegation.

What happens when we deal with Millennials who have different expectations of the work place? We know they want to be given responsibility, flexibility and a belief that what they do in the work place adds tangible value. Does it change anything?

My personal belief is that it should be easier to delegate to a Millennial than to a worker from an older generation, because at the very start of the delegation process you enter into a discussion about the "why, what and the how" of the project that needs completed. This will resonate with the younger generation who seek clarity and a sense of purpose in their work. Consequently, they would be encouraged much earlier on to 'buy-in' to the importance of the task and will see how critical their role is in helping its conclusion. Establishing regular touch-points so they can report back on the project, but at the same time allowing them freedom to "fill in the gaps" between those milestones as they see fit, will give flexibility and responsibility to that employee.

I hope you would agree that delegation is therefore probably the most important skill to develop as a great manager, so if you are on that journey you should definitely learn how to do this. However, I've already mentioned that many managers don't know how to delegate so it is quite likely that when given a task or project you will have this dumped on you without it being communicated to you in a way that will support a successful on time completion. Why do you think so many large projects fail to deliver when they say they will and are rarely as originally specified or even on budget? Now how about turning this on its head and consider how you could utilise the process of delegation in such a way that you help your manager to delegate to you rather than the other way around.

STEEL FIST OR VELVET GLOVE

It is the start of another busy week in the Tendering Department and you are looking at the pile of work on your desk wondering if you will ever be able to go home at the end of the day. David, your line manager, calls you over to his desk. "Abigail," he says, "I've just the job for you. The Directors have decided we are going to buy Johnsons Consulting just up the road and they want it all signed and completed in two months' time. Sort out what we need to do to make this happen and let me know if you get stuck."

You return to your desk and wonder what you are going to tackle first.

Does that sound familiar? You've just been dumped on and realistically will this all get completed on time and in the best way? I think that's unlikely. We could consider the situation in a different way, one where you are in control and manage the situation to ensure that this task is completed efficiently and on time. Using what you know about effective delegation, let's run this again:

It is the start of another busy week in the Tendering Department and you are looking at the pile of work on your desk wondering if you will ever be able to go home at the end of the day. David, your line manager, calls you over to his desk. "Abigail," he says, "I've just the job for you. The Directors have decided we are going to buy Johnsons Consulting just up the road and they want it all signed and completed in two months' time. Sort out what we need to do to make this happen and let me know if you get stuck."

You respond with "that sounds really exciting David, but could I ask a few things so I understand exactly what it's all about?" David puts down his pen and looks quizzically at you. "Go on then" he says.

"I just wondered why it's come into our department and not legals because we have loads of work to do. Not that this is an issue, I'm just curious."
"Good point Abigail. Basically Johnsons have loads of tenders in place and if we secure these by taking over the company, it has the potential to grow the company by nearly 30%. Our understanding of tendering makes us best able to get the people at Johnsons on side more quickly."

"That's great David and when do we need it signed again?"
"Two months from today please, apparently we cannot miss the deadline because there are a few other companies looking and we have first call. If we miss the deadline, we won't get another chance."
"That makes perfect sense, but why do you think I'm the best person to get this done?"
"That's easy, you are the most organised person I know and you've done something similar at your last company. I know because your last boss spoke very highly of you after you left there."
"I appreciate that, and of course I want to make sure we do our best. If nothing else, it will make the department look good, but am I to work through this by myself?"

"What's bothering you, Abigail?"

"Nothing much, it's just I've got four tenders I'm currently working on and I wouldn't want to mess up on this take-over, it seems really important for the future of the company. Would there be any scope for me to pass some of the other work across to Johnny so I can concentrate on this job and get it right first time?"

"I think we could do that."

"Thank you David, now can I discuss some of the details with you, so I fully understand everything before I get started?"

So, Abigail has positioned herself as being the right person to do the job and has created some time to work on it. Without being difficult or insolent, she has taken control of the conversation and is now getting engagement from her manager. As well as obtaining all the information she may need, she is now about to establish a firm plan to start the project.

"Is that enough information for you, Abigail?"

"Yes I think so, but I'm sure if I need anything else I can come to you. On that note, shall we arrange a 15-minute catch up every Friday, say at 3p.m. so I can update you on where I'm at?"

"Yes of course, but do we need to meet every week?"

"I may need to speak to you in-between then, but I just think that keeping you updated is important, in case the bosses ask you how it's going. In addition, I also I think I'm going to need help at some stage, probably from HR, from the Legal Team as well as from I.T. If I need them to spend a day or two with me, I'll need your help to facilitate them being let go to come here."

I'll not carry on with all of the story as I'm sure you can imagine how Abigail would have the full support of David and access to all the resources she may need. On completion of the project on time, how do you think David would think of Abigail now? What if this was you? You've just made him look brilliant. I know for certain that he will see you as a strong ally and want to help you succeed more quickly. Is that less or more likely to help you progress in the company more quickly?

Delegation, therefore, may be the MOST important skillset for effective management, but it is not the **only** thing you need. Apart from being a good delegator, you will need to be able to think effectively on your feet as well as being able to make decisions and stick by them. The first one is a skill that can be learnt and the second is just something you need to develop confidence in.

Let's deal with the first point – the ability to think effectively on your feet. So, I'll bet that most of you don't play chess but you probably have a general idea of how the game goes. Basically, each player has sixteen pieces made up of eight pawns and eight higher pieces; two castles, two bishops, two knights, one queen and one king. The pieces are moved around the board in order to "take" the other players pieces. In order to win the game, you need to consider how you will move each piece around the board to get them into a position where they can take one of the opposite players' pieces, eventually resulting in all the pieces being taken or a situation where the King is unable to move without being taken, which is called check-mate.

When planning where to move the pieces, this often involves thinking about three or four pieces at the same time, and also one or two potential moves each piece can make. At the same time, you need to think about the possible responses and moves the other player could make. You may be pleased to know that this is as far as I wish to take how the game is played, but the analogy is important. To be an effective and quick thinker you need to think like you are playing a game of chess. Consider multiple scenarios of how your team will perform a task or project. Ask yourself "what would happen if they did this or I said that?" Now change the scenario and think it through to the end. What happens? Is this the result you want? Change the situation again and work it through, again. Note that all of this is **before** you have actually made any decision. Stephen R. Covey in his book "*7 habits of highly effective people*" tells us that one of the key traits is to **begin with the end in mind**, so what is the best case outcome you are looking for?

> ## "Employees who believe that management is concerned about them as a whole person - not just an employee - are more productive, more satisfied, more fulfilled. Satisfied employees mean satisfied customers, which leads to profitability."
> **Anne M. Mulcahy**

You are probably wondering why you should spend so much time planning and thinking about what may happen when in reality you will probably not use one tenth of what you have considered. A good point and one with which, in principle, I agree with. However, half of the possible scenarios will be discarded by you as they won't achieve the result you require. Of the remainder, you now have a number of possible routes to getting the solution you desire. So roll forward to when you need to decide on what is to happen. Having pre-thought it through, you are able to pick one of the solutions, knowing that if everything plays out the way you imagined, you'll get the result you want. Oh yes – and you made that decision quickly, or at least it appears that way to those you manage. They will be impressed and have confidence in your decision, making it more likely the solution will work out the way you planned.

Well guess what, "Murphy's Law" being what can go wrong will go wrong, invariably occurs. When it does, your team will look to you to think of another solution and make a decision. The advantage you have is that you have already pre-thought about the situation and so can be decisive, which strengthens the conviction of your team who will do as you ask without question; and subsequently achieve the desired outcome.

So what is the alternative? Don't bother doing any pre-thinking and allow your decisions to be made on the hoof. Your team will look to you anxiously while you think out the possible situations. You will appear indecisive and unsure, and every unplanned hesitation, minimises the confidence and trust your people have in you.

So what do you do when you get thrown a curve ball and you haven't had time to pre-think the situation? There are three ways to recover such situations, but knowing they will occur at some time and that you are good enough to solve the problem, should make you generally more confident and have a stronger belief in yourself.

Buy yourself time:

The first thing you need to do is to buy some time to think the situation through so you can come up with a solution and make a decision. You have plenty of time, but at all costs you need to appear confident to your team, as there will always be someone looking for a weakness, a chink in your armour that they could potentially exploit. Be strong and fair in everything you do, but above all, don't panic!

So how do you buy time? Simply, it could be the time it takes you to finish a hypothetical phone call and walk through to the other room, or perhaps you could say you'll "just get a coffee and be right there". It will be rare that you need to make an instant decision, but if you do, developing the right mind-set will give you the tools you need to find a solution and show yourself to be someone who can, and does, think effectively on their feet.

Ask your team:

So the problem with the high altitude position you feel as a manager is the mistaken belief that you have to bear all the responsibility yourself. Now don't get me wrong, the buck stops with you for now, but that doesn't mean you have to stand alone in everything you do. In fact, being aloof is not going to engage your team in any way, but rather quite the opposite.

Firstly, don't be afraid to think that asking your team for their thoughts or opinion is a sign of weakness, because it isn't. After all, you don't actually have to blindly follow what they say, but the key here in engaging your team is to ask them and then to sincerely consider what they have said before you make your decision. This is fairly basic stuff if you have to manage Millennials. I explained earlier that they want to have a say in how the organisation is being shaped. They want a voice and for that voice to be heard and listened to. Ignore this at your peril as imposition of your way without consideration of all the facts is unhelpful at best and disastrous at worst.

> ## "Most of what we call management consists of making it difficult for people to get their work done."
> ### Peter Drucker

Dr. Ivan Misner, Founder of BNI® is renowned for saying that "diplomacy is the art of letting other people have your way" and from this we understand that by helping your team to believe it's their idea you are following will encourage them to buy-in and deliver. The important factor is to simply listen properly to what your individual people and collective team have to say, carefully consider it and then **always** tell them why you have or have not gone with their idea or what they have suggested. Above all, never be dismissive, as sometimes your team are closer to the issue than you are and have a different insight to the problem. All the information, no matter how small, is relevant. Remember that a 1000-piece jigsaw is incomplete without all the pieces.

Now, having gathered all the information it's time to make that decision. Whatever else you do, be decisive and confident, even if it turns out to be the wrong decision. All you need to be able to do is justify <u>why</u> you made the decision. If you have gathered all the information possible at the time and carefully considered your options, then you will in most cases have made the right decision.

What do you do however if you have got it wrong? Well let's take the example of a large oil tanker sailing through the ocean. The Captain makes a decision to change course to Starboard (right). Due to the size of the ship, it can often take ½ mile from the helm being turned to achieve a perceptible movement in the bow and then a mile or two of travel through the sea to complete the manoeuvre. Hypothetically, a short time after starting to turn, the decision is found to be unsound and a return to the former course is required. The order to change course back again is given and the helmsman is told to turn to Port (left) and does so. On the principle above, it can take ½ mile of travel to stop the movement and steady the course, followed by ½ mile to start the movement of the bow in the opposite direction. Even if the ship returns to its original bearing, it may now be running a few miles away from the original course – i.e. parallel to it – so an over-correction is required to get back on course. A bit more effort is required but it is not an impossible objective.

"Truly successful decision-making relies on a balance between deliberate and instinctive thinking."
Malcolm Gladwell

What lesson, then, am I trying to impart? Quite simply, changing a decision can be easy; getting back to the direction and course you were on before may not be. Take care on the decisions you make, but be confident that you make those decisions based on all the information you have at the time. If the decision turns out to be wrong later on, then don't try to reverse the decision because you can't – but you can get back on track! Always remember the analogy of the tanker at sea; that your course is decided upon and, although not easily changed, it can be, as being on the wrong course is not necessarily critical. Reconsider all the information you <u>now</u> have and make a NEW decision, set a different course and be confident in that decision. Above all, do not be tempted to make knee-jerk actions as they will invariably go wrong because they have not been thought through. In gaining the information you need, don't fear asking your people for their thoughts – they will actually appreciate you more for it. Use their knowledge of similar experiences to guide you in your judgement. How did the last situation work out? If it was a bad outcome, then don't do the same again. If it was good, then what worked before in similar situations will probably work again, just make sure you have considered ALL the facts before taking action upon your decision.

You now have some new-found wisdom – how will you apply it? My recommendation is that you learn from those around you and consider many different scenarios. When you do this in your decision-making activity and you gain more confidence, you will develop the ability to pre-think those situations, just as with the pieces on the chess board. Once you do this, then the next time you need to think quickly you only have a choice of what action to take, without all the thinking to do that goes with it.

Finally, if you are the employee or part of the team, how will you support your manager in making those decisions? Adding value and being seen as a confidant will make you someone to be relied on for thoughtful, sensible input. It's not just about the recognition; but rest assured, you will soon become the key person, the one who is relied upon as the 'go to' person. If you are seen in that way, who do you think will be asked to step up while your manager goes on holiday? The employee who adds value and is supportive, or the individual who just does the bare minimum? Seize every opportunity you can get to show your management capability as not only does it give you practice, but it will get you noticed for all the right reasons.

Chapter Thoughts and Actions:

• Ask yourself, what type of delegator are you and consider how adjusting the way you currently delegate can achieve greater results?

• How can effective delegation make a difference to our engagement of employees and in particular millennials?

• Don't be proud and think you know it all – ask your team and learn from their experiences and knowledge.

• Display your confidence when making decisions and gather all the facts before deciding – your team will follow if they see this in you.

Chapter 7

DEVELOPING PERFORMANCE

There are a number of key things that most managers dislike having to deal with. Disciplining an employee is one, absenteeism another, and then we have performance. In this chapter, I'm going to deal with the latter because, if handled well, the other two will become less of an issue. However, to be effective it should be approached in a positive way rather than a negative one: in a manner that motivates and encourages rather than one which disenfranchises the employee.

Another misconception is that when you commence a performance process it is only as a means of criticism or punishment, eventually leading to the termination of the employment. In other words, it is seen as inevitable that the employee will leave. As I explain later on, this is not what your Performance Review Process should be about. Developing performance is about achieving an improvement in the employee in relation to specific areas where they need it. Notwithstanding that continued failings may result in that person leaving, but this is not the primary intention.

> ## "The main point is to get the right people on the bus (and the wrong people off the bus) **before** you figure out where to drive it."
> ### Jim Collins

I've spent many years looking at various ways to develop performance, from 360-degree feedback systems, peer-review processes, formal annual appraisals, carrot-and-stick methodologies, role evaluation calculations and complex online, as well as paper-based systems; all claiming to be the most effective way to engage and motivate your people.

When considering this, the most common expression I hear is the word "appraisal". This puts the fear into a manager that they will now have to spend hours of their time trying to remember the good and bad from the previous 12 months, write it down and then confront the employee. At the end of this, they ultimately decide whether they get a pay rise this year or not. Does this sound familiar?

The problem with appraisal systems are that they are usually just a part of a tick-box exercise which has little or no value to the organisation or the employee. They are backward-looking as it is all about what has been done by that employee in the past. It usually has a poor scoring system and, worse still, is often linked to annual pay rises based what the employee has done well over the past year. They are subjectively based and if the manager does not particularly like the employee, then a lower score will often be achieved, which in turn could affect any pay increments. To add insult to injury, the manager often spends considerable time they don't have, putting together some carefully crafted words that are delivered "at" the employee. Due to the poor recording of good and bad things that have taken place since the last appraisal, the manager may often have little information beyond the previous 6 weeks (memory dependent) and so give a skewed and inaccurate representation of the employee's performance. Appraisals are usually perceived by the establishment as having little or no value and are dreaded by employees and management alike, meaning that they often go to the bottom of the 'to do' list. The ownership and control lies with the manager who may be pestered by employees expecting their annual appraisal because it is linked to a pay rise. In my opinion, appraisals therefore dis-incentivise and demotivate.

> **"When you are talking about the contributions of hundreds or thousands of individuals, what you're really looking at is a very broad spectrum that goes from the bare minimum that an employee will do to avoid getting fired to the very best job that a person is capable of. The difference in productivity between those two polar extremes is astronomical."**
> **Frederick W. Smith**

Performance development processes, however, are forward-looking and all about what the employee is going to do in the future. I would much rather have employees thinking how they can improve, stretch, inspire and develop, instead of just assessing something that occurred in the past that cannot now be affected. That aside, we need to learn from our mistakes and failures so we can improve going forward; consequently, some review of past performance is necessary. In taking this approach, I much prefer the use of a three-page document which places a large amount of ownership on the employee and is far more effective than pages and pages of irrelevant history. I will explain a little more about this document later on. The key, however, is that the process should not only align the focus of the employee's performance with the goals and objectives of the company, which should achieve the desired results, but should do so with the minimum of management and employee time.

However, the important factor that is required for the development of good performance to work effectively, is that the company must understand what its own overall objectives are and communicate these to the staff. The difficulty is that in many cases the business owners and CEO's don't actually know themselves, especially in smaller organisations. Ideally, businesses need three things to inspire and inform their people as well as the wider community who may use their services or products. They need to have Mission, Vision and Values. Now I don't want to stray too far into Leadership as this book is about managing people, but feel I should touch on this here because managers also have a critical role in displaying attributes of positive leadership when necessary. In its simplest form, this is about helping to support and epitomise the company's core values, encourage commitment to the mission and help to inspire belief in the vision. This is as important when developing effective performance with the objective of aligning the employee with the direction the company is heading.

I spoke earlier about personal values and also how these shared values could be extremely powerful at an organisational level, but more importantly they shape the culture and strengthen the core philosophies of how the people should behave. If the people don't share in the company values, this can create conflict and they won't align with the mission or believe in the vision. Recruiting or developing the right people with the right mind-set that aligns with the company culture and values, is less likely to result in issues. Part of this requires the organisation to be business savvy to start with, and to have a clear mission about what it does, to who it does it, and why.

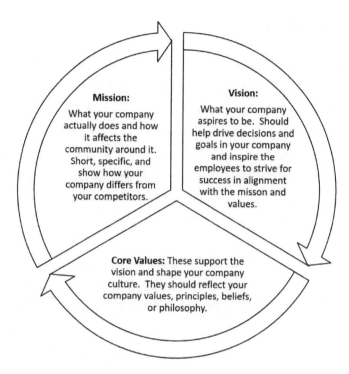

How powerful would that be if this was communicated to all employees and they bought into the mission, believing how the company they work for intends to serve the local community or society in the wider sense. Would that resonate with those who are seeking a place to work that shares their own values? What if the CEO of the organisation showed they were a great leader and communicated a vision, that inspired employees to want to still be around to share in the future benefits to come, where everyone worked in harmony being aligned with the core values and mission? Perhaps those employees may genuinely feel empowered to help the organisation achieve its very purpose.

Let me give you an example;

Stacy, the newly-appointed Marketing Assistant, was set a goal to complete the copy for the new website. This had to be completed within three weeks as the new website was critical for the latest product launch and the company had paid for an advertising campaign to commence as soon as possible to drive extra traffic to the website, thus generating new sales. The new product launch was important for the company as this would allow it to be less reliant on its current existing product offerings.

The deadline was missed due to the website copy not being in place and a Performance Review meeting held. At the meeting, Stacy admitted failing to complete the copy without giving any real reason for this. Recognising that perhaps the "why" had been missed, Peter – her Reviewer – talked about how this new product was going to place the company at the forefront of the latest technology. Having a successful launch meant job security for everyone and a great deal of kudos for the company, and by inference, anyone who had contributed to that success. It would have been very easy to take a strong stance and possibly discipline Stacy; however, in talking about why it hadn't been completed she was able to explain that she had struggled to finish the work due to not having been trained on how to upload the information into the web-site. Stacy had nearly completed the actual copy but fallen at the last hurdle. A new objective was set to get training from the web-company and to complete the copy.

Now the critical part: a date two weeks from the review was set for completion and a further meeting put in the diary to discuss that single objective. In a normal review, other past goals and objectives, and any future objectives, would also be discussed at the review meeting; but for now, let us continue with this single objective that was set regarding the web-copy. At the meeting two weeks from the review, Stacy will have achieved one of two things; either improved her performance and got the job done, or failed again. She had completed the work and was praised for a job well done. As a consequence, Stacy is now more engaged with the performance process as she understands its use to achieve small steps towards a larger goal.

Business Objectives <u>and</u> Desired Direction for Employee

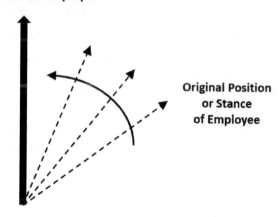

Original Position or Stance of Employee

This is the most effective use of the performance process where the employee is incrementally aligned with the direction and goals of the business. Ultimately, if the employee chooses not to change and continues to conflict with the company's objectives, then the outcome of ongoing failures to address performance may result in disciplinary action. However, it should not be the first objective. Remember the potential costs to losing an employee from the business and having to replace them – so why would you not want to at least try to resolve poor performance? Offering support at every opportunity will usually encourage a change in behaviour from the employee, and combining this with training where required gives the employee every chance to engage in achieving a positive outcome. Where it doesn't, then quite simply the employee is making a decision that they do not wish to align themselves with the goals of the organisation. This fundamentally places the responsibility of whether the employee stays or leaves the company in their own hands, and they now have a simple choice to "*Shape Up, or Ship Out*".

> ## "In the minds of great managers, consistent poor performance is not primarily a matter of weakness, stupidity, disobedience, or disrespect. It is a matter of miscasting."
> ### Marcus Buckingham

This is effective for dealing with one task, but what about on-going failures or an overall general decrease in performance. Unfortunately, I've found that many managers believe that the way to manage employees that are under-performing is either through disciplinary sanctions – i.e. written warnings up to dismissal, or to operate a tick-box process of appraisals every year, because that's what they've been conditioned to do – and both methods fall short of the reasons for doing this in the first place.

If we take disciplinary action as a first option then it is clear that the process is just being used to get rid of the employee. This should <u>never</u>

STEEL FIST OR VELVET GLOVE

be the initial objective with poor performing staff, as everyone should be given an opportunity to make mistakes and learn from them. Repeatedly making those same mistakes or just not making any effort – now I fully agree that is a different story. Annual tick-box appraisals, on the other hand, are a waste of time and effort as they rarely improve and motivate the team, being linked to pay and having no real substance. Utilising a well-formulated Performance Review Process is the best way forward to help engage and motivate the employee.

The key behind delivering an effective performance process, however, is a willingness from both parties to discuss what is happening; to be open, truthful and to agree objectives going forward, whether these be weekly, monthly, quarterly or annually. I mentioned earlier about the document I like to use to help facilitate this. The document has three sections on the first page comprising of Past and Future Objectives. On the second page are a list of Key Competencies but with two "scoring" columns, one for the reviewer and one for the employee. The third page is for Reviewer, Employee Comments and any Actions, Training or Support that have been identified during the review.

In the first section, those objectives or goals that were set at the last review are listed and a discussion about how well these were reached, or not as the case may be, takes place. This must be an open discussion about what went well and how any failings can be improved next time. The discussion over the past objectives is the opportunity for the employee to discuss why a particular goal or target was not reached, and from this discussion, future objectives and any required actions are created. New goals and targets are listed, some which may have arisen from the past objectives and others because the business or role has changed. These future objectives may have arisen from the past objectives which need reassigned or adjusted – or brand new ones – but most importantly, a date for completing or achievement is set and both parties held accountable on this date.

To make the second part really effective, it is vital to recognise that its purpose is not to "score" necessarily, but for the Reviewer and Employee to assess where they think the other is in their development. The employee needs to bring their own self-assessment of their performance to the review. If the scores 1-10 match or are really close, then no action may be needed except to discuss how this could be improved. Where there is a differential, this is the point where a discussion about why and how the scores differ takes place. The critical factor is about each party being honest with each other regarding the review process as a means to improve.

The third part is for general comments to be made by both parties and detail any support or training that has been identified. Here's a story from Ian Kinnery who sees the value of the Performance Development Review as critical not just for his clients, but in his own business too. As a World Class Business Coach, European Coach of the Year 2007 and owner of Team Massive Results, he has been "developing the owner to grow their business" since 2006 and prides himself on finding the best way to engage his clients to make a decision and take action.

Some years ago I asked Alasdair to run a Masterclass for my coaching clients. I had become convinced that the biggest single, often unvoiced, fear among SME business owners and leaders was how to exit people from their business. As part of that first session, Alasdair introduced a Performance Development Review document as a means to realign an employees' effectiveness or, if they failed to step up, remove them.

As a business, one of our core values is that we eat our own dog food; which means that we walk our talk. We have an express intention that we provide an example that we would want our clients to follow. If I am recommending a process or a practice that I myself don't follow then, in my eyes, that makes me a hypocrite and why would I expect my clients to listen to a hypocrite? Consequently, I sought to absorb Alasdair's performance review into our own management processes.

Whenever I have a client who is complaining to me about a member of their team, what they have done, or what they have not done, once they have finished their rant I will ask the same question: "Tell me, if your team member was a fly on the wall and had heard what you had to say, would they recognise themselves in the description you have just given?" Without exception the answer is "no they wouldn't". Why? Well, as business owners and managers, we tend not to have those discussions anywhere near as often, or as openly, or as fully as we could and should, usually because such conversations can be difficult.

It strikes me, however, that the majority of conflicts arise when one party has a very different opinion of the performance and behaviour of the other party, than the other party has of themselves. It really doesn't matter who is right or who is wrong; what matters is that it ends up as an unspoken and unresolved difference, a difference that can never be resolved unless – and until – it can be put on the table openly and without judgement and discussed.

So we started to use the Performance Development Review document Alasdair had provided. We were awkward at first but like everything it improved with repetition and practice. Each time we carried out the review, we began to customise the core skills and competencies section. We felt that it was more useful to have attributes, or even attitudes, as well as skills that were specific to the individual and the job. If a heading was no longer relevant, appropriate or it became unnecessary, we changed it.

In my mind, the real value of the document is the dialogue that it catalyses. As a starting point, we individually scored our own sheet and only when we got together would we see the other persons' scores. We also created an open environment where we would discuss the two columns of scores, one from my perspective, the other from my employees'. Then we looked for the categories where we had a significant difference in scores. That forced the question, "why is it that you have scored yourself a 7 when I have scored you a 5"; or "why is it that you have scored yourself a 7 and I have scored you a 9?" That way, none of us could be in any doubt about the opinion of the other.

This process allows us to have the discussions that we would not otherwise have. It forces us to be honest about what we are doing, how we are behaving and how well we are performing. In reviewing each score we challenge ourselves as to whether they are as high as we would want or expect? Are we in agreement about what the categories mean and why they are important and still relevant?

As we have repeated this exercise and turned it from an event into a process, the effectiveness of which has multiplied. I am a big believer in the importance of rhythm and the part it plays, so we have incorporated this discussion as part of a quarterly rhythm. In other words, it happens four times a year. Consequently, it no longer feels so strange or strained. It is just one of those discussions that is central to the smooth-running of our business and that happens on a prescribed rhythm. We don't do it because we have to or because we feel we ought to, we do it because it works. Repetition just means it works better each time.

The whole thing also feels less remedial, being much more about improving our performance and about working better together; so much so, that the last few iterations of the process have led quite naturally to both parties setting stretch goals for the next 90 days that would not otherwise have happened.

The amazing thing I have found is that it allows both parties to have a full and frank conversation about performance without any threat, which in turn allows the individual to take an interest and an ownership for their own development and performance. The benefits of that are outstanding. Once that happens, the individual will not only own their performance standards, but they will care about them too and realise that those standards really matter to them.

When we use 'Role Descriptions' as part of the review process, my belief is that the most important part is where we describe the main purpose of the job. That should be a very clear and precise *summary of what the job is all about and should never change unless the 'Role Description' changes. We actually cut and paste the main purpose of the job into the review document, so it is there for us all to see and to remind ourselves what the job is really all about. This allows us to draw any and all conversations back to the core purpose.*

Additionally, we have aligned the individual questions with the Core Values of the business, which makes the review process much more of an alignment tool. Consequently, we have noticed that over time the targets and goals have become much more aligned to the strategy of the business. The quarterly rhythm dovetails quite naturally with the quarterly strategic planning rhythm. That isn't to say that it has to happen at the same time but it does form an integral part of the rhythmic heartbeat of the business.

Utilising an effective review process can therefore help with the part of the manager's role which is to strive for good employee engagement. This is very important as we know that engaged employees work harder, are happier at work, and contribute a higher level of creativity towards the development of the organisation. It seems ludicrous that many business owners marginalise the value placed on helping create a more engaged workforce, as the benefits outweigh the effort required to achieve this. It does, however, require an approach that understands there is more to the process than just focussing somebody's goals and objectives in order to align them with the organisational mission and vision. Engagement covers the employee's sense of belonging to the organisation, such that the employee feels they are valued and cared for. As a consequence, they will give more in return. This is especially prevalent for the Millennials Generation as they will give more of themselves to an organisation that promotes a sense of purpose that aligns with their values. As an aside, the responsibility does not totally lie with the manager or the organisation in achieving this. If you are one of those Millennials and want to be understood more, then you need to seek ways to create dialogue to explain what you want and what your values are; otherwise the manager may approach you with their perception of you, which could be totally wrong.

Now, one of the main difficulties for many businesses is how to assess the engagement of the employee and, once measured, how to improve any areas that are not at a high enough level. However, there is another way to do this, through the utilisation of the "Thrive Model", which considers seven main areas that assess how well an individual or organisation as a whole is engaged. Emma Barugh, who runs a successful HR Consultancy, MBHR Limited, has many years' experience in large blue-chip organisations where she focussed on the art of staff engagement. It is perhaps fitting then that Emma's business specialises in employee engagement and that she has developed "Thrive" into an effective online tool for doing just that.

Emma shares with us her story of how she met Paul McGee (The SUMO Guy), which then lead to her developing the Thrive Model with him. As Emma tells us, employee engagement is critical to organisational success, yet is not as complex as it may at first seem;

> *I firmly believe that when opportunity presents itself, strike whilst the iron is hot. I listened to Paul McGee speaking on stage at a CIPD event. It was my third time of hearing him in person. On this occasion, he was sharing his conversational Thrive Model for employee engagement, which is based on the*

"Seven C's": Clarity, Competence, Confidence, Comfortable, Cared-for, Challenged & Control. Now, Paul's passion lies in public speaking, and when I spoke to him after his presentation, he expressed little desire in developing the Thrive Model into an online system that could be accessed by companies and business owners to develop and increase their employee's engagement.

His focus was in continuing to write books and to speak on stage. My passion, on the other hand, is about engaging employees and increasing their well-being. What I clearly saw that day was how easily Paul's Thrive Model could align itself to the UK's Health & Safety Executive's Stress Management Standards. If such a tool could help employees to miss 43% less days through ill-health, then what a more enjoyable workplace could be created – and the advantages of that for those organisations that embraced Thrive would be a considerable increase in profitability.

Over the next few months, I spent some time with Paul to work out the finer details and a business model to sit behind an online tool for the use of the Thrive Model. Interestingly as with any good idea, to do so brought its own challenges and obstacles, and I had to constantly work at remaining positive, engaged, aligned and focussed on my end goal.

As I explored deeper into the seven C's that form the Thrive Model, I realised that I had been applying aspects of this on an intuitive level in my previous work, and long before I met Paul. An example of this is when, shortly after I moved companies to a different job and role, I acquired a new team.

I discovered that one of the employees, who had over eight years' service and a reputation for poor performance, had never undergone any form of performance management process throughout that time. He had no understanding of what was expected of him and it appeared the company had minimal understanding of their expectations of him. Rather than take a direct stance and consider whether a disciplinary process was necessary, I started communicating with him to create a framework which gave him "Clarity of Purpose". An almost immediate improvement of his output was observed and it appeared he was on the journey to showing his true potential.

The next thing that I felt was holding him back was his "Confidence" and, along with that, his own self-belief. I made it my objective to get to know him personally, while at the same time striving to find out from a business perspective what his needs and wants were. I then sought to praise him when he did good work, utilising a ratio of about 5:1 "praise versus criticism" as this is known to be the most effective way to reinforce the adage of "catching somebody doing something right and tell them they are doing it". As a consequence, his self-belief in his own capabilities made an immediate and marked improvement too. Had I known at the time about the other five aspects of Thrive, my conversations with him could have been so much more powerful. Even without discussion around these additional facets, he continued to improve and went on to become a top performer, eventually achieving promotion.

So that sounds very simple and implies that it is not necessary to utilise the full benefits of the Thrive Model. Let me tell you how the Thrive Model works and then judge for yourself:

© Copyright Paul McGee, PMA International Ltd

Thrive works on the basis that an individual, team or organisation, should be seeking to achieve green in all seven areas. Those sections where they are not green, instantly indicates areas that can be tackled to gain improvement. At its most basic level, the Thrive Model can be used to facilitate conversations exploring each of the seven C's one at a time, as part of the continuous conversation, or as part of a more structured performance management process. Thrive can also be used as a means to provide insights at an organisational, directorate, team or functional level.

I am particularly enthused by the Thrive Model as it is underpinned by relevant theorists both old and new, in the field of motivation, engagement and well-being, such as Maslow, Herzberg, Yerkes-Dodson, Prof. Cary Cooper and Stevan Hobfoll to name just a few.

To give a deeper understanding of how Thrive can be applied to an individual employee in the organisation, we need to explore each of the seven C's with the individual, as below:

- *__Clarity__: How does the individual's core purpose and values align with that of the organisation? Does the individual understand the organisations' vision, mission, values and strategic objectives? Do they understand where they fit in? Have the organisations' expectations of them in their role been fully and clearly communicated and explained?*

- *__Competence__: Does the individual have the skills and knowledge to undertake their current role? What about their next role? If not, does the organisation facilitate the necessary development of them? Can they attain what is expected of them, with or without supervision? Do they have the self-belief that they can pursue their career within the organisation and ultimately achieve a level of self-actualisation?*

- *__Confidence__: Does the individual receive appropriate,* *motivational, constructive and inspiring feedback, praise and recognition? Does this impact positively or negatively upon their confidence? Does this affect their performance?*

- **Comfortable**: *Does the individual understand the organisational culture? Are the behaviours they observe in their leaders, managers and peers consistent with the organisational culture or at variance? Does the individual trust in the senior management, direct line management and their colleagues? Is the culture experienced by the employee consistent and aligned with the culture the organisation displays?*

- **Cared-for**: *How does the employee feel about their emotional health & wellbeing at work? Do they feel the organisation gives appropriate consideration to their mental health within the workplace? Does the individual feel they can rely on their management and colleagues for support when work, or their personal life, is emotionally demanding?*

- **Challenged**: *Does the employee feel challenged at work? Do they have meaning in their work and are they given meaningful work to do? Does the individual enjoy the level of variety that exists in their role or does it create conflicting priorities? Do they have too much, too little or just enough to do?*

- **Control**: *Does the individual feel they have sufficient influence over how, where and when they achieve their work? Are they granted appropriate levels of responsibility and flexibility to achieve the tasks set?*

The key is to seek a balance across all areas in accordance with the HSE Stress Management Standards. If one area is dramatically out of sync, then this is an area for concern. After all, one can be satisfied, motivated and engaged; but if one's health and well-being is undermined then, try as they might, they will not be capable of performing at their best.

The Thrive Model is a powerful tool that can be used from the very first contact with a prospective employee through their on-boarding process and throughout their career with the company. The adage that you should "recruit for potential and attitude, and train for skill" is an effective and common-sense approach to building and developing effective employees. I passionately believe that if you find the right people, then ensure that each of the seven C's are developed within every employee and integrated into every day communications, then this will create an amazing place to work, where the employees and organisation will thrive.

A powerful opportunity to keep employees engaged and a tool that could be used for the effective performance management of your employees as well. However, sometimes a stronger stance is required when things don't go according to plan and the employee chooses not to engage. This is where the decision over whether disciplinary or performance management is necessary needs to be considered.

If you remember earlier, I mentioned about the cost to replace good people. So, let's consider one of our employees – let's call him Michael – who has worked for the company for 10 years and he starts to make mistakes. All too often, the initial action is to invite him into disciplinary and issue a first written warning or worse still to ignore it altogether! He continues to make mistakes and under-perform and because this irritates you, he gets pulled in for another disciplinary to explain himself. As you are dissatisfied with his answers, he gets another warning; this time a final written one. Michael is resentful that after so many years of loyal service, he is being disciplined and, consequently, is unwilling to tell you what is really going on. Being demotivated, it is not long before he makes further mistakes, resulting in a final disciplinary and his termination of employment. This is a fairly typical situation, but unfortunately all that has happened is that a previously good employee, who has given much to the company, is lost. The likelihood is they will get another job doing the same thing but now it's for your competitor and he can pass on the knowledge he has of your company. Restrictive conditions post-termination are hard to enforce and if the new employer doesn't ask for a reference you cannot even tell them you fired him. All in all, it is a sorry state of affairs.

> **"Success in business is all about people, people, people. Whatever industry a company is in, its employees are its greatest competitive advantage."**
> **Richard Branson**

So let's rewind a little to the point where Michael's performance starts to slide. First of all, as a good manager, being aware of how your team and individual employees are performing at all times is a skill worth developing. Then, the next stage is to hold an informal meeting with Michael – just a chat, over coffee perhaps – and ask him what is going on. You don't need HR involvement at this stage and, as his manager, you have the right and obligation to look after the welfare of those you are responsible for. It's not prying, it's managing! Be sincere and point out that you have noticed he is not himself and his performance is slipping. It's quite likely he'll appreciate the fact you are interested. Then ask what is causing this and if there is anything you can do to help. Every employee is a valuable asset, and if you can bring him back to his former level of performance (or near to it) then you retain his skills and knowledge.

Now the very act of asking creates a number of outcomes;

1. The first is that you find out that there are some issues at home (financial, domestic or illness) and although you may not be able to help, or are requested not to, the very fact of showing concern and offering will help Michael realise that working for you is a good place to be;

2. The second may be there are issues at work (such as bullying or stress) that you can support or intervene on and resolve, because you cannot allow underlying issues such as these to fester. The outcome could be a claim against the company for not doing something to stop it;

3. Or the third may be that he is just ready to move on, either to progress his career, a career change, or retirement – in which case, supporting him will ensure he remains on your side. Loyalty is hard to keep after someone leaves, but you and Michael should not be ready to burn your bridges as there are many cases of good employees leaving a company only to come back at a later date.

Now the main objective gained by taking an interest, is that if you are able to support Michael with either of the first two issues, then the impact of these factors is minimised. The positive result is that Michael returns to his former performance level, no further action is necessary and he is grateful you took the time to bother.

The second outcome is that Michael says there are no issues at all, offering no explanation for his failings. If this is the case, then you have given him the opportunity to seek help, which may be support from the company through training and a change in role, hours, location etc. The next steps however – and you must make this clear to Michael – are that continued failings in performance may result in a **formal** performance process. Again, let him know that you are there to support him if he wants to discuss anything. Now, critically, do not forget to document the conversation, ensuring the file notes are placed on his personnel record; otherwise when you need to deal with a similar problem in the future, your ability to remember in any great detail will fail you.

Continued failings from Michael may result in one or more informal discussions, but eventually you will need to implement a formal performance process. The notes you made earlier are now invaluable as your evidence of his underperformance. Now the obvious outcome of Michael not achieving the targets and goals agreed upon will be a first written warning, and continued failure of the same issues to the next stage leads to a final warning, with a potential escalation to eventual dismissal. At every stage, you must offer support to Michael, additional training if needed, and explain the consequences of his continued poor performance. If finally dismissed, the fact that you have a documented process which Michael has ownership over, and support has been provided at every stage, will give him nowhere to go. It is regrettable but inevitable, and Michael may decide to leave before he is dismissed, hence the expression *"Shape Up, or Ship Out"*.

Now, in practical terms, the performance process must be meaningful, and the objectives set must be bold enough to challenge the employee to stretch themselves. That is why agreeing these in the meetings between you and the employee will ensure they have buy-in to the objectives. In other words, they have not just been arbitrarily set by management. They should also not be so hard to achieve that they demotivate the employee who will not even try in the first place. The actual process should be carried out over a discussion taking 10 to 30 minutes (maximum), and the employee should be encouraged to bring their desires, objectives and goals to the meeting. This may include a desire to attend developmental training courses and, provided there is some ROI back to the organisation, such should be encouraged and supported. Furthermore, in carrying out the process, I have found three questions to be the most effective to get the best results, when reviewing past objectives and setting new future ones, as listed below:

1. What actually happened?
2. What should have happened?
3. How can we make this better?

The use of these questions challenges the employee in a positive, aspirational way, and allows for a meaningful discussion and the re-setting of new objectives. Please, however, remember to set a date and stick to it, otherwise the whole process is undermined and becomes something that the employee doesn't trust. The result is disengagement from the business.

Chapter Thoughts and Actions:

• Do you know what your business objectives are – mission, vision and values?

• Have you communicated this to your people – if not, how can they know if they are doing the right things?

• Do you have employees who are disengaged and not doing the best for the organisation and if so, what are you going to do about it?

• Disengaged employees operate at half their capability – how can you manage them differently to get an improvement in productivity?

Chapter 8
THE 3 R'S

Most of us think about the 3 R's as **R**eading, w**R**iting and a**R**ithmetic and although perfectly valid and important, in the context of people management, I find that **R**eward, **R**esponsibility & **R**ecognition are somewhat more relevant. So, let's deal with these one at a time.

Reward

Despite popular belief, "pay" is not just about the money. In fact, it's actually about everything to do with remuneration. This includes the monthly or weekly pay check, the Christmas bonus and other commissions, as well as some of the less tangible benefits you may have available with which to reward your employees. However, many people do not consider the other less obvious ways in which individuals and members of the team can be rewarded. Such things are the extra half-day holiday which you don't deduct from their annual allowance, or everyone going home a few hours early one day because a project got finished on time and within specified requirements.

Perhaps it's you bringing everyone some doughnuts or cake to have with the morning coffee as a way to say thank you for the efforts that have got you recognised by your boss for doing a good job. Another really great way to reward the team and help them to work more as a more closely-knit team is to celebrate birthdays and take everyone out for a "Birthday Breakfast" treat. It doesn't have to be lavish, but meeting up somewhere before work and paying for it not only helps with team socialisation, but also makes everyone feel good at the start of the day.

You might even find the team are happier at work and give a little extra as a result. The alternative is to create an environment of fear at work where people feel uncomfortable. This will only drive the employee to clock-watch and do the minimal amount of work to get by. They will be generally unhappy at work, not communicate effectively and always be looking for the next opportunity, not how they can best do the job where they are. This is even more critical for Millennials who crave recognition, a level of flexibility and, most importantly, to be part of a community. Those social media peer-to-peer sites are not successful by chance, but because they resonate with a particular generation. Creating a social community with the workplace is more likely to retain employees when they have a bad day because they no longer feel isolated and can seek solace with those in their own peer group, just like they do on their smartphones.

You may not be able to keep your best employees forever, but you want them to give you 100% all the time they are with you. Spend the time nurturing them, give them reason to appreciate they are in a great place to work so that they will be more predisposed to grow and stay with you longer and give you their best efforts all the time.

> ## "The grass isn't greener on the other side, it's greener on the side that you water it."
> **Dr. Ivan Misner**

Of course, in the HR world, the phrases "flexible-working" and "work-life balance" are bandied around as the best way to have happy and motivated employees, but that is not always achievable. In reality, many businesses, especially smaller ones, don't have the ability to cater for such extras as they are often too stretched with resources or just not geared up to have flexible

STEEL FIST OR VELVET GLOVE

hours. However, as a good manager, recognising when a hard-working employee needs to get away a few hours early for an appointment or an issue at home, then creating the space to cover for them, will earn you a huge amount of respect from that person. The art in doing this, however, is to not do it too often or worse still only favour one employee; yet if you master this it can reap huge rewards in return through extra effort from the employee. As human beings, we are hard-wired to reciprocate, but it has to be given freely and not begrudgingly to start with. So, if you have the ability to not dock that half-day holiday or make them take it as unpaid leave, then that will boost employee motivation to another level. However, here's the cautionary bit; it's a two-way street.

"We make a living by what we get, but we make a life by what we give."
Winston Churchill

What does that mean? Quite simply, ask yourself if you are the employee who arrives at exactly 9.00a.m. and takes every minute of your lunch break at the same time every day, ensuring that at the end of the day you wash your coffee cup at 5.15p.m. before leaving bang on 5.30p.m.? You would be right to say that is what you are paid for, but give some thought to how those around you think of you.

Discretionary effort is the difference between the amount of effort you are capable of bringing to an activity or a task versus the lowest level of effort required to get by or make do. If you are serious about developing your managerial ability, this will only happen if you stop thinking with an "entitlement" attitude. Show some initiative and look for things to do that will help the company be more successful. Treat those around you as you yourself would like to be treated. Getting to work slightly early so you are sat at your desk working at 9:00a.m., asking if it's a good time to grab your lunch and working up until home-time before putting your coat on, will get you recognised by those who will influence your career development as well as those you may eventually be responsible for. Would you like them to be motivated and respectful of you as a great manager, or conduct themselves in the mirror image of you? I've said it before, but "behaviour begets behaviour"; just understand that it is your choice as to how others view you!

If you are already a manager and you have an employee who clock-watches, you are probably wondering how best to deal with that particular situation. My recommendation is not to get cross but to ask them why they behave in this way. Then look inwards and ask yourself, "what expectations were established with them when they started?"; "Has anyone spoken to them about what working as part of a team actually means?"; "Is there a reason they need to leave at exactly 5:30p.m.?"

As someone from the Baby-Boomer or Generation X age group, this may appear like some of your staff already, unwilling to go the extra distance which is extremely frustrating! Worse still, they just happen fit into the Millennial Generation and now you can label them. I hear the exasperation in your voice as you declare to anyone who will listen, "we know all about the problem with Millennials". They have no work ethic, wanting to come and go as they please, they have no respect, won't commit to the business and want more money for doing less. I also hear your protests that your staff aren't willing because they tell you, "you don't pay me enough, why should I do more?" Well, do you know what? You are probably right – but then again, perhaps you aren't.

Have you asked your employee how they think about their job, what they believe would be acceptable attendance times, what they actually want in their role? Do they want to develop themselves, become a team leader perhaps, or even progress into management? Instead of complaining, we need to take responsibility of this situation and stop making assumptions.

Ask your employee those difficult questions, but do so in a non-threatening way by being sincere and genuine. Ask them to help you understand how their generation think, so you can help shape the future business such that everyone will benefit. When, and if, they give sensible answers, then spend the time explaining how it actually works in business, that patience is a critical factor in an individuals' success, and that staying for the long-game instead of wanting it all right now is the best way to be. It will be much more effective to motivate and engage your team in this way as they will develop a sense of purpose, which is actually important for everyone from any of the generations. Share your vision and values of the company, align their thinking with the future – as beyond any doubt this generation will be our future leaders and managers. We have to help them to help us shape the businesses of the future, ones that are relevant to them and which can be run more efficiently, effectively and profitably by them.

And to you – yes, you, the younger employee looking to develop in your role and aspire to the heady heights of being a manager one day – what are you doing to help the above take place? I mentioned it was a two-way street. That means you have to try to understand how the older generation think and why they act as they do. Show them why they should value your youth, creativity and energy. Help them to understand you and, as a consequence, you may just understand them in return. Creating a commonality of understanding can only result in positive things.

> "The most important role of managers
> is to create an environment in which
> people are passionately dedicated to
> winning in the marketplace."
>
> **Andrew S. Grove**

One thing I didn't mention above was handing out pay rises. These are always welcome, but apart from the Public Sector, even cost-of-living pay rises are not guaranteed. In the commercial world, margins are forever being squeezed and sometimes the profit is just not there to hand out. In addition (admittedly I'm being a little contentious here), a pay-rise is useful for about 3-months as a motivator and, following the passing of that period of time, the employee will probably just be broke at a different level, as most will spend what they earn and secure extra credit for the things they can't afford! Make sure, then, that if you are awarding pay rises, they are meaningful. If you want to create an aspirational motivated culture in your business, then reward your people for effort and excellence, not just for doing their job.

Responsibility

Apart from rewarding your employees financially, how else can you motivate those exceptional individuals and team members? Promotion is one option, provided the person is capable of doing the role and you are not just falling into the "Peter Principle" and promoting above their level of competence. To clarify, it should not just be about bestowing a title on someone. Instead, it should be about ensuring those who get promoted firstly deserve it; secondly, they can do the job competently; and thirdly, that when they are promoted, they will add value to the role with which they have been entrusted.

Therefore, if responsibility is not about promotion, then what is it? I believe that responsibility can be shared out in small doses and have a positive motivating effect on the team and the individual. Most employees want to have both meaning in their work and meaningful work to do. Going home at the end of the day and feeling that you have done your best that day, and in some cases actually made a difference, gives us all an indefinable internal reward. If you think this is not the case, then ask a nurse, police officer or fireman why they do what they do every day for the money they get paid! Fundamentally, it is a basic human need to be recognised for the good things we do, and when we are, it creates a great sense of satisfaction and well-being within us. Ask those employees you know who are motivated and they will probably tell you that what adds to their self-worth and self-esteem is when they are recognised for being capable of that extra-important task and are then asked if they will do it.

I have spoken with many demotivated employees who have commented that their manager could be so much better if they would just ask them for help. Now please be careful – I don't mean keep dumping extra stuff on that person just because they are good at it, you will wear them out and in turn that will exhaust and demotivate them. In addition, if they are always doing your work, then perhaps when the boss gets to know about it, you may be redundant and the employee gets promoted into your job. Learn to delegate effectively, and I urge you to read my chapter on that if you haven't already done so.

In considering what I mean by sharing out a little bit of responsibility, let me give you an example of how you might do this, just by asking in the following way:

> *"John, I have a really important report to put together for the presentation to the Board tomorrow. I appreciate I'm asking at such short notice but I'd really value your input on this as I know you excel at our stock control system. I need a couple of presentation slides and some notes to be able to highlight the need for us to upgrade the system. I'll make sure I mention your help when I discuss this with the boss. Can you find the time to help and if so, would you be able to help me out?"*

If you notice in the way I presented that to John, I took time to edify his skills making him feel proud then I asked if he was not only willing to help but also had the time to do so. Finally, I made a point of telling him that he would be mentioned as having an input, which ensures he gets the recognition he deserves and you haven't claimed all the glory. I personally detest managers who take the credit for other peoples' efforts. Not only is it morally wrong, but it's the number one way to demotivate the individual. Furthermore, as everyone else gets to know that you claimed the glory for someone else's work, the rest of the team are demotivated and unwilling to go the extra distance too. Conversely, making the point that you got help from within your team will show your business leaders that you understand your peoples' skill set and value. Being prepared to ask your team to help shows that you are not concerned that someone in your team may be recognised as better at something than you. In fact, the opposite occurs and, if done right, the boss may actually mention it to John the next time they meet. Now, how do you think that will make John feel?

Finally, when you take time off, have you identified who will cover for you? Who in your team has shown the aptitude and attitude to do this and do it well? As a Tutor Constable in the Police Service, one of my jobs was to help train new police officers, who were fresh out of training school, in the art of policing on the streets. Many of those I mentored rose to headier ranks than me, but that was fine. Had I not recognised and nurtured each of their particular qualities and had instead tried to suppress the individual from doing better than me, then I would not have been regarded as an exceptional tutor. It did help that Durham Constabulary's mission statement was *"Aiming For Excellence"*, which was exactly what I aspired to do, all the time.

Now I will admit that to help others grow beyond you requires a deep-seated confidence in yourself and your own capabilities. Believe and trust yourself and stop seeking those "brownie points" for everything you do. As you develop into a great manager, the recognition will follow.

I was told a story recently of a company that had a brilliant manager heading up a really good team of people. The manager was so good it looked to his bosses like he did nothing. So, they decided to make him redundant and manage without him. All of a sudden, the best performing team wasn't doing so well, and after a while, a number of them left the company. The bosses eventually challenged the remaining members of the team and asked why things were not working as they had been before. The answer was simple; the manager they got rid of because they thought he did nothing actually ensured everyone was motivated, accountable and kept on track. He made things happen, he handed out responsibility to individuals which they relished in, and he spent the time constantly and consistently rewarding and recognising their individual and team worth.

> ## "When people are financially invested, they want a return. When people are emotionally invested, they want to contribute."
> **Simon Sinek**

Recognition

On the subject of recognition, this doesn't necessarily have to cost anything and can be something you can deliver to the individual, team or even companywide, easily and effectively. That will be great news if you are a small business on tight margins, but what might this look like?

One obvious way would be to have an *"Employee of the Month"*, where you post their photograph around the business. If you are in retail, this also shows the public that you recognise your team for their successes, and after all, we like to see people be recognised. It makes the individual feel good too, doesn't it? The difficultly is that this is true up to a point, right until it gets over-used like so many things. For it to work effectively, it should be done in a sincere and genuine manner.

Having placed an individual on a metaphoric pedestal, how might you keep the rest of the team motivated? The simplest way is to use the time allocated to the team meeting where the individual is rewarded with the accolade and tell the rest of the team the things the person did to achieve the goal. These need to be the things that everyone else could do if they put in that little bit of extra effort, so they can believe that becoming *"Employee of the Month"* is something they could achieve too. Communicating this effectively will serve to encourage others to give a bit more of themselves or seek to do the one exceptional thing that deserves the recognition.

However, do this positioning badly and it will demotivate instead. Occasionally, giving the award to the less-able, or the team underdog, for one outstanding action can also have a very powerful effect by not only raising the confidence and determination of the less-able employee, but also spurring the others to be better too.

The younger generation love recognition, almost to the point that they crave it. It is critical that in developing your managerial capability, you recognise that their need for instant gratification and recognition is greater than ever before. If you don't believe me then take a look at how many people clamber to have their thirty seconds of fame on radio or television programmes. They appear oblivious to the idea that they might fail, despite the fact that they are often being set up for a fall in the name of entertainment, which serves only to impact negatively upon their self-esteem, creating other issues. Given this knowledge and in order to be an effective giver of recognition, great care must be taken. It requires thoughtfulness, consideration of the impact it will have, must bolster confidence and a responsibility to teach everyone else to be pleased for the recipient, yet hungry to receive the accolade themselves.

It should also be noted that handing out recognition in the sales environment is much easier as this can be based simply on targets achieved and exceeded. It is a fairly straightforward "give" and always well-received because the typical nature of sales people is to strive to be at the top. Unfortunately, the downside is that their personalities usually expect a monetary reward for doing so. Notwithstanding that, even when they just get told they are the best that month, they will be motivated regardless; as after all they like the attention.

However, I have found the most effective way to motivate people through recognition is when it is not done publicly, but is done sincerely and directly to the recipient. To become a master in giving recognition, requires you to understand differing behavioural styles as this is the way you can maximise the impact of the recognition, because the way you say it to the individual is different in each case. Now, there are many behavioural, personality, strength and other psychometric assessments available, but I personally like DiSC® as this is simple, easy to understand and, in most cases, people can remember what the assessment said about them. This means that they are much more likely to take action and use what they have learnt. So how do you develop an understanding of DiSC® and a person's behavioural style?

Allow me give you a little bit of history, first. In 1928, a psychologist called William Moulton Marston in his book "*Emotions of Normal People*", further developed the work of Dr. Carl Jung on the way in which a person's emotions can impact on the way they behave. The different types of emotional expression were categorised by him as **D**ominance, **I**nducement, **S**ubmission and **C**ompliance. In the 1940's, a great deal of effort was being made to develop a way to measure behavioural types, and industrial psychologist Walter V. Clarke developed a list of adjectives for employees to select that they felt best matched themselves. In doing so, he discovered that these fell into a similar framework as that discovered by Marston. In the early 1950's, in a desire to reassess the emotional attachment that employees gave to their work, John P. Cleaver wanted to directly evaluate employees against the jobs they did. In conjunction with Walter Clarke Associates, Cleaver developed what is now known as the DiSC® Personality Type System for determining behavioural types. The different behavioural types have been slightly renamed over time to become **D**ominance, **I**nfluence, **S**teadiness and **C**onscientiousness; and there have been many variations since.

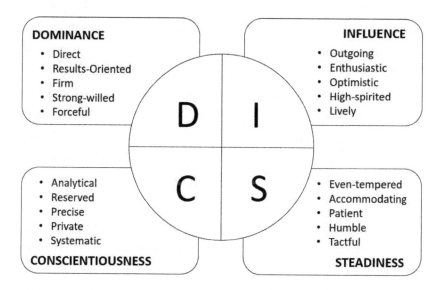

DOMINANCE
- Direct
- Results-Oriented
- Firm
- Strong-willed
- Forceful

INFLUENCE
- Outgoing
- Enthusiastic
- Optimistic
- High-spirited
- Lively

D   I

C   S

- Analytical
- Reserved
- Precise
- Private
- Systematic

CONSCIENTIOUSNESS

- Even-tempered
- Accommodating
- Patient
- Humble
- Tactful

STEADINESS

What many people fail to realise is that we actually have parts of all four aspects within us, and that it is only the "dominant" type that is most prevalent. This is therefore the one that everyone would recognise in another and the one that tends to encourage an emotional reaction in a person. Each of the different types can still surface, however, depending on the situation – so should not be ignored. However, playing to the main strengths is what we aim to do when handing out recognition, as this is the one to which the employee is most responsive.

Now this is all very clever stuff, but assessing someone's behavioural type just by looking at them is not so easy. That said, if we could understand how people behave before we spoke to them, and then interacted with them in a way that more readily matched their behavioural type, it's reasonable to believe that this will make them more responsive to what you say to them.

Asentiv® (formerly *Referral Institute®*) teaches the utilisation of such understanding to help business owners generate more business through relationship marketing. If you are interested and wish to gain a greater insight into this, I would highly recommend *"Room Full of Referrals"* by Dr. Tony Alessandra (a world-leading expert on this subject matter), Dr. Ivan Misner (Founder of BNI® and Co-founder of Asentiv®) and Dawn Lyons (Co-founder of *Asentiv®*). What I particularly like about this book is the redefinition of the DiSC® terminology into different names such as; Go-getter (**D**), Promoter (**I**), Nurturer (**S**) and Examiner (**C**).

These are an easier grab on the terminology and such that most people will more readily understand what each of these behavioural types looks like at work. I expect that you are rather sceptical and don't really believe me. Okay then, let's give it a try. Who in your work place do you know who is a real Go-Getter? See what I mean – and I'll hazard a guess that was fairly easy for you.

> "You have to get along with people, but you also have to recognize that the strength of a team is different people with different perspectives and different personalities."
> Steve Case

Knowing this, how might we utilise such knowledge if we want to give recognition? To help you, I'll explain a little about the different behavioural types and then describe some ways in which you might give some effective recognition to each of them.

Go-getter

This is the person who can appear, at times, abrupt, dynamic, fast-paced, but definitely not focussed on the details. Instead, they are focussed on getting everything done, yesterday! If you try to explain anything in detail, they will interrupt to try to help you get to the point sooner. After all, time is money. They are quick to make decisions and if they are the CEO, it is often "my way or the highway". They want all the information in a half-page report; anything else won't be given the time of day. They are high achievers, want to be the best at what they do and crave recognition.

Promoter

These type of people are busy-bodies, always asking about other people and their business. They can be seen as a bit nosey sometimes, but effective promoters will glean information sometimes without the other person realising it due to the manner in which they engage with them. They "know" everyone and everything, which is why they are effective networkers and the go-to person if you need to connect with someone else. They love talking and will use any excuse to do so over a coffee rather than get the work done.

Nurturer

These people are the carers, they are instantly sympathetic, and rush to help someone who appears in distress. They are the person that people go to when they have a problem and want to talk it through. They like to "mother" their colleagues and are loved by everyone, but this can result in conflict when the go-getter asks why they are not getting the work done. The response from them is usually one of indignation as clearly there are more important emotional issues going on.

Examiner

For these employees, it's all about the detail. They apply painstaking effort to ensure everything is perfect. There is no "it's nearly there" or "let's go with it as it is" with an examiner. They can often appear shy or aloof, not necessarily because they are but rather that they are just focussed on the task in hand. They are also usually cautious about letting their emotions show except where they are criticised about the accuracy of their work.

Now as you can imagine, this is just a snapshot of what the various different types of people could look like. Of course, there are many other ways to describe behavioural styles, but I'm sure you can think of people you work with that fall into one of the above as being their main dominant characteristics. So, if we are to give recognition, understanding what their dominant behavioural style may be can help us as a manager to be more impactful.

For example, if we learn to recognise the different types of people we manage and then get an opportunity to tell one of the team that they excelled at something, it might sound like this:

Go-getter

> "Hi John, just need a moment with you to say thanks, the report you sent me on the sales analysis was fantastic. I really liked the half-page summary on the front page that saved me a lot of time searching through the details. If you can do that again on the next one that would be really appreciated."

Promoter

"Jenny, could I just get a few minutes with you. I just wanted to let you know how pleased I was with your efforts at the product launch event. I noticed everyone seemed to be enjoying themselves and that you were mixing well and connecting the right people with each other. Mr Johnson was particularly complimentary about how you looked after him. I just wanted to let you know how much I appreciate your efforts and wondered if you'd like to be involved on the next event?"

Nurturer

"Hello Brenda, thank you so much for your help the other day when we got the news about Peter. I know it hit the team quite hard but I noticed you gave just the right amount of support to everyone to help them put it into context. I don't think I could have got the team back on track as quickly without your empathy. I really appreciate you looking out for us all and if you can let me know if anyone has any issues so we can support them through those. Thanks again."

Examiner

"Mark, I just wanted to let you know that the detail you included within the accounts, in particular the part on our projected ROI was of immense help when I presented to the board on Tuesday. They threw some pretty tough questions at me and I was just thankful to have all the answers. It's good to have you on board and let me know if I can do anything for you in return."

These are just some examples of how the conversations could go, but I recommend that use your own words and style, varying what you say. Focussing on the particular language that appeals to the individuals' behavioural type will make them feel better about themselves. Do you think people recognised in this way would be less or more likely to help you in the future?

Julian Lewis is the Global Brand Ambassador with Influencers, who works with many companies to help them develop strategies for their people and business success. His experience working for blue-chip companies such as BT, Sony, Tyco and Galileo, has afforded him the necessary insight as to how important understanding the people within a business, and helping them to better understand themselves, is critical to delivering effective solutions. As part of this, he strongly encourages business owners and managers to start influencing through the understanding of behavioural styles based around the DiSC® system.

To enhance this further, he encourages people to discover their reason "why", and in doing so supports business owners and managers to develop themselves. The following story illustrates how his understanding of behavioural styles, combined with an individuals' reason "why" was transformational for one of his clients.

> *I was working with Keith, who was responsible for all health and safety in the organisation where he was employed. Keith was a quiet man who was very efficient in what he did but he never really seemed happy in his work. I decided that I would get to know Keith and spend some time with him to see how I could get the best from him in his work.*

We discussed what he did for the company and Keith described it like this; "I do the minimum that is required by legislation, in other words I cover off all the tick boxes and forms. Nobody likes doing this, but I don't mind and I'm good at it, so I get it done for people even though it is seen as dull and a necessary evil." It was clear to me that people did not respect the work that Keith was doing, and because of this Keith was not enjoying his work.

His behavioural style is that of a high C in DISC terms; or an Examiner; or what we in Influencers call "Blue". Keith enjoyed getting all the little bits of details correct so that the company was fully compliant with their legislative requirements. It satisfied his need and his behavioural style so it was important not to take this away from him, as to do so could create internal conflict and confusion.

I was however troubled that Keith was so unhappy in his work, so I asked him one question, "why do you do what you do?"

Now, unsurprisingly, the initial answers were quite unsatisfactory, especially to me. They included comments like, "because it needs to be done" and "because I am good at it", as well as "the law exists so we have to get the boxes ticked". Both of us were getting a bit frustrated as none of these answers felt right. I decided Keith was holding back on something, so every time he gave a vague response, I countered with, "no Keith, that cannot be it, please tell me why do you do what you do?"

I needed Keith to come up with the answer himself, to give the real reasons, not what he thought I and others wanted to hear. Keith, who was actually a little upset with me at this point, then said, "I do it because I want Fathers and Mothers to go home to their children at night!" Wow – that statement hit us both like a blinding flash of the obvious, but until then we had not been able to see it. Keith lit up and his whole demeanour changed immediately. The next time I saw Keith he was a different person. He had been telling people how important his work was and his colleagues had been agreeing with him. As a result, they embraced what was needed and were even doing far more than the minimum required by the law, all so that fathers could go home to their children every night. Keith was now able to concentrate on using his skills to get the detail right, which also fed his desire to keep people safe.

As an employer myself, I wanted to make sure that I had a strong understanding of what really motivates people beyond money and I found this within Keith's story. Keith went from doing a job for the money because it had to be done, to being a key part of the business where he had respect and was held in high regard, all because he found his "why" and realised how his behavioural style impacted on those around him. I was also able to affirm that this type of work suited Keith's behavioural style, such that he was comfortable doing the work and not in conflict with himself.

As a consequence of the exploration I carried out with Keith to discover his reason why, combined with an understanding of how his behavioural style drives his work, I now fully comprehend the importance of the mix of these two factors in helping people to be the best they can be. This is why I'm committed to helping as many people as I can to light up and find fresh motivation.

Understanding someone's personality type can clearly help you interact with them in a positive way. With Keith, it was to develop his understanding of himself, so he could make a difference to others and at the same time feel aligned with his purpose.

The ability to adjust and align yourself with the behavioural style of someone you are interacting with makes the difference between that meeting being positive or negative. The ability to build rapport quickly is an essential trait, whether you are helping someone grow their business, motivating them to be a better employee or just in your everyday interaction with people.

As a manager, or aspiring to be one, being able to assess an employee's behavioural styles will allow you to engender greater communication with them. By adapting your communication style to match your language and physiology with them will create rapport more quickly whilst encouraging the employee to feel better about themselves. Many managers, however, feel that it is the responsibility of those around them to adapt their behaviours to them. That's because they see their role of manager as one of "controller" or being "in charge", which gives them the right to demand and tell others what to do. Perhaps that's why so many managers are just no good at it?

To be controversial, I'd like to challenge that perspective and suggest that it is actually <u>our</u> responsibility to adjust how we communicate with employees, not the other way around. The human species is a social creature and we are attracted to people who are of a similar ilk. People like those who are similar to them. As an effective manager, being more aligned in our communication with an employee will generate a more positive response from them.

The final aspect to be adopted when we utilise the 3R's as part of our managerial tool-kit, is to ensure that in every case we should try to encourage an individual to discover their "why". In doing so, the individual gains greater clarity about themselves and we glean an insight into what drives those we manage. With such knowledge, we can adjust the delivery of reward, recognition and/or responsibility towards the individual, and achieve greater motivation and productivity from them.

A win-win situation.

Chapter Thoughts and Actions:

• Recognise that everyone has a dominant behavioural style that makes them behave in a particular way towards others.

• How can you utilise your knowledge of the different behavioural styles to help support individual engagement?

• How might you change your own language and behaviour with an individual, to more easily motivate them and get them on your side?

• How will you adopt the 3 R's as an effective way to motivate your team.

CONCLUSION

How then does this book help us to be more effective managers; or if we are just starting out, to help us to accelerate the journey? Its simplest goal is to hope that there was a story, an analogy, a technique that has created a flame of thought within you that you feel you could take away and try on those you engage with. If there is, please reflect on what took place; could you have a handled it better, said it differently, changed the way in which you delivered the message. What would that have looked like if you had?

Recognise that you will never know everything and can always learn something new. *"Every day is a school day"* and you must constantly challenge yourself, learning as you go and expanding your toolbox of techniques. The more you have at your disposal the easier it becomes to choose the right one, at the right time, to get the right result.

> ## "Learning is experience, everything else is just information."
> **Albert Einstein**

Never be scared to make a mistake – it's the way we as human beings have achieved so much in such a short space of time. However, do not just keep making the same mistakes over and over. The fundamental premise of this book is to give you small incremental ways in which you can test and measure how they work for you. We learn more quickly through experiential learning than being shown how to do things. The following analogy may help you understand the difference between WISDOM and EXPERIENCE.

A man is walking along a forest path. In front of him, he sees a tree root sticking up out of the ground and as he steps over it he trips. As he lands on the ground he bashes his nose and it bleeds. "That was painful", he says to himself, "I won't do that again." This is EXPERIENCE.

Another man is sitting on a nearby tree stump watching the man walk along the forest path. He sees him stumble and fall after tripping on the tree root and says to himself, "I won't do that in the first place." This is WISDOM.

However, later that day, the second man is walking along a different path and sees a tree root sticking up. Remembering what he had seen earlier and applying his new-found wisdom, he says to himself, "That is a tree root, I should be careful so I do not trip". Alas, he still catches his toe as he steps over the tree root and falls to the ground. However, as he does so he is able to break his fall, and apart from being a little dusty, is unharmed.

Now I hear you cry: what use is wisdom if it doesn't stop us from making mistakes. However, to truly learn, we must experience. The difference is that, by developing wisdom, we reduce the magnitude of the mistake.

Your role as a manager is to develop your own skills, knowledge and attitude so that you can be the best **you can be** and get the most out those you are responsible for. If you communicate effectively and considerately, those employees will want to give more of themselves. Sharing the values of the business with them will align them to that purpose and they will become

STEEL FIST OR VELVET GLOVE

more engaged in what they are doing. Remember, I have mentioned the Millennial Generation many times already. By 2030 it is estimated they will form over 60% of the workforce. Understanding that these future managers and leaders operate on a different construct to those from earlier generations, because the world has moved on, is essential if we are to prepare them to be the best **they can be**.

> # "100 years from now, no one will care what house I lived in, what car I drove or how much money I had in my bank account. The only thing that will matter is whether or not I made a difference in the lives of others."
> **Alasdair Ross**

It is your mission to develop your abilities so you can support and encourage those individuals that are looking to work for businesses that offer a sense of purpose, are flexible, creative, fun and where they can have a voice that is impactful as part of their own future. Is this worth the effort or not?

I would strongly urge you that it is. The difference between a disengaged employee who is marking time at work, and one who is committed and engaged as an integral part of the company, its mission, vision and values, is around 75% – what would that look like in monetary terms? Would even empowering your staff and getting even a little more from them willingly make a difference to your business and its future? Even more importantly, when you are no longer around, what will you be remembered for?

Your intention to be a good manager that looks after your employees and clients is the first step along this path. It starts with your values which need to be shared with as many people as you interact with. Develop a strong vision and a positive mission statement, but most of all, once done, communicate this.

In this respect just how do you communicate your values and purpose to your team? Is that one shared by the company? Do you have the skills to delegate and engage those you are responsible for, through strong, fair and consistent management? How and why you do this will shape their commitment to working with you. Your ability to positively manage them and help them to stretch themselves means that you will have influenced a person to be better than they were before they met you. Now that is a legacy I want to leave behind. What about you?

As I am committed to making a difference and 'walking the talk', I have developed a Mission Statement for We do HR Limited which aligns itself with that ethos. All my employees share in these values which focus on honesty, integrity and delivery of exceptional service. We make a difference and live by the principles within this. I feel it relevant to have included my Mission Statement for you:

"By providing comprehensive support and passionate caring consulting, we solve your people problems and foster positive employee engagement. We do HR does this through honesty, integrity and fairness, with purpose, to effectively motivate your employees allowing your business to achieve a thriving culture and ultimate success."

Therefore, if we manage others in a fair and consistent manner, through the analogy of the *"steel fist, or velvet glove"*, where we value our employees yet show ourselves to be strong for them, the opportunity to take some pressure out of the workplace is in our grasp. The Health and Safety Executive claim that 9.9 million work days were lost through work-related stress, anxiety and depression in the UK in 2015! That does not count those people who are too scared to go on sick leave for fear of losing their jobs. Imagine a world where employees feel less pressure, less stress, generate more productivity and are generally happy in their work.

There is no doubt in my mind that a more engaged workforce is only achievable through a change in management behaviour away from one that is over-bearing in its nature. This requires a conscious acknowledgement by all managers and leaders that bullying in the workplace is unacceptable and a desire to do something about it.

"Unfortunately, it's also true to say that good management is a bit like oxygen - it's invisible and you don't notice its presence until it's gone, and then you're sorry."
Charles Stross

There is a wonderful expression that I feel sums up how we should behave all the time and it is, *"How you do anything is how you do everything"*. We cannot change the past nor can we live in the future; however, in the present moment and the immediate future to come, we can affect what the outcome of the longer-term will look like. Your interaction with everyone you meet sets the path for that future time. A simple change in your attitude affects everyone around you so when you wake up, or when someone hacks you off, just ask yourself how you intend to be for the rest of the day. If you try to be upbeat and positive, smile a little perhaps – it can be infectious. As a manager of people, you will impose your attitude and behaviour onto your team. If you're happy and motivated, they will be too.

Thank you for reading this book. If you are a manager or aspiring to be one, I hope you have taken something from it that you can use to make a difference. If you are a business owner that employs managers, then I ask you to look at your team and see if any of those fall into the sub-35% bracket and are bad managers. Carefully consider what you will do about that, what impact is it having on your organisation? Above all, I implore you to encourage all of your people to strive to improve in their daily interaction with those they work with and manage more effectively.

WHAT'S NEXT?

If you have enjoyed this book and would like to know more about how you can develop effective managers within your business, or would like to know how you can develop yourself to be a great manager, then please contact me via the different means below.

If you would like to give something back to me, then a good referral would be:

- Buying a second copy of this book and giving it to someone who may choose to be better at how they communicate with others; or
- A warmed-up introduction to the CEO of a business that would like to develop their existing managers or start to grow their future leaders and managers. My sister company, We do Learning & Development Limited has bespoke development programmes to achieve exactly that; or
- An opportunity to speak to groups of people who may be interested in changing their future to make a real difference.

Contact:
    Email: guru@managethefuture.co.uk
    Twitter: @managethefuture

Lightning Source UK Ltd.
Milton Keynes UK
UKOW06f1549200517

9 781910 406649